If the U Fits

Expert Advice on Finding the Right College and Getting Accepted

Kevin McMullin

and

Robert Franek

The Princeton Review
111 Speen Street, Suite 550
Framingham, MA 01701
E-mail: editorialsupport@review.com

© 2014 by TPR Education IP
Holdings, LLC.

ISBN 978-0-8041-2471-3
ISSN 2332-1210

Senior VP—Publisher: Robert Franek
Editor: Kristen O'Toole
Production: Best Content Solutions,
LLC

Printed in the United States of America
on partially recycled paper.

9 8 7 6 5 4 3 2

2014 Edition

Editorial
Robert Franek, VP Test Prep Books,
Publisher
Selena Coppock, Senior Editor
Calvin Cato, Editor
Meave Shelton, Editor
Kristen O'Toole, Editor
Alyssa Wolff, Editorial Assistant

Random House Publishing Team
Tom Russell, Publisher
Alison Stoltzfus, Publishing Manager
Ellen L. Reed, Production Manager
Dawn Ryan, Managing Editor
Erika Pepe, Associate Production
Manager
Kristin Lindner, Production
Supervisor
Andrea Lau, Designer

For Rosie

The consummate Collegewise fan

Table of Contents

Introduction

col·lege ['kol-ij]
noun

1.   An institution of higher learning offering undergraduate studies that lead to a bachelor's degree (also "university" or "U").

2.   An academic superstore offering undergraduate students four years of learning, growth and self-discovery.

3.   Move-in day, professors, rush week, lectures, road trips, rallies, the big game, debates, concerts, majors, minors, turning 21, all-nighters, spring break, graduation day, proud parents, next steps and fond memories.

Foreword

After 20-plus years of working in college admission, my daughter received her PSAT results and I found myself in a situation I never imagined: I was consulted on standardized tests while at home, brushing my teeth (and yes, it is difficult to respond with authority while doing so). I thought my work experience would grant my family immunity from the crazy pressures of the college admission process, but wow, was I ever mistaken. Even in our house, fear would creep into every spare moment between the release of those scores and the day my daughter decided on her school. I now know that it does not have to be this way.

One of the perks of working in an admission office is that I am surrounded by truly good people every day. My colleagues, at my own institution and throughout the higher education community, care deeply for kids and their dreams and about improving the world through education. I came to meet the founders of Collegewise through a colleague at The Princeton Review, and I think their blog, www.wiselikeus.com helped me and my wife survive the college admission process. The blog is free, and it's a delight to read, just like *If the U Fits*. We found it to be a powerful antidote to the anxiety.

I often reflect on a conversation from my final days of high school. I was cleaning out my locker and I bumped into a former teacher who asked the question that seniors hear all too often: "Where are you headed to college?" I answered, and he was obviously disappointed. "Oh, anyone can get in there," he said, as if the chances of admission somehow indicated the quality of the institution. I went on to have a wonderful experience: I met amazing people (including the wicked-smart, beautiful, incredible mother of my PSAT recipient), I received an excellent education, and I am a part of a worldwide community of which I am very proud. I am happy in my life, and I know my college choice is a big reason why. Yet even with all this, many are still baffled about why I turned down schools they see as better choices. I am so glad I ignored them all, and my wish for any student is to feel just as good about their choice, wherever that is.

This book will bring peace to the process. You will learn how to maintain a sense of control. You will better understand how college admission officers think about candidates. You will learn how to build a list of colleges that focuses on real qualities that will benefit the student, not on the perception of prestige held by others. In the end you will likely have several options, and you might even have a hard time choosing a school to attend. If you do it right, your family will grow closer together, your child will leap toward adulthood in a healthy way, and you might even be surprised to discover new things about the student you have raised. You have the power to take on one of life's major transitions, a transition that will affect your whole family, gracefully. Enjoy the ride, for it is indeed a thrill.

Kirk Brennan
Associate Dean, Director
Office of Undergraduate Admission
University of Southern California

The views expressed here are Mr. Brennan's alone and do not represent those of the University of California.

Introduction
How to Approach the
College Admissions Process

Before coming to Northeastern, I wouldn't have even been able to dream of the opportunities it has created for me. I would have never known what I wanted to do, I would have never known what it's like to live in a city, and I'd definitely never have gained the life experiences that will inevitably help me in the future. This college changed my life.

Wes F.
Former Collegewise student, Class of 2006
Northeastern University

Early starts

Two weeks before I left for college, I wrote a 10-page instruction guide that I boldly told my 15-year-old brother had everything he needed to know about getting into college. Most of the promised wisdom came from hindsight, things I'd have done differently if somebody had told me (or if I'd ever bothered to visit my high school counselor to ask for advice). At the time, *even take the SAT Subject Test in biology right after you finish taking the class in 10th grade* felt like sage college counseling advice.

Three years later, my brother got into Harvard.

Granted, he was class valedictorian and a state champion rower. I'm sure his credentials influenced his admission more so than the printout from my Apple IIC did. But the guide was my first foray into what would eventually become my career. Today, my brother is a Harvard graduate, my mother keeps that guide in a box of family mementos and I run a college counseling company, Collegewise. As of this writing, my team of counselors and I have helped more than 5,000 students get into colleges they're absolutely thrilled to attend.

I was inspired to start Collegewise while working for The Princeton Review, where I presented to high school students and parents about the SAT and ACT and the role of standardized tests in college admissions. The audiences were wound tighter than my hamstrings at a yoga class. No lasting good was going to come from reminding them how many applicants with perfect SAT scores get rejected every year from Princeton. So I brought a different message: relax—nobody's ever become a failure in life because of their SAT scores.

I also learned that the public's focus on the most prestigious colleges meant that most of my audiences knew almost nothing about less-famous schools. If I asked, *Does anyone know the average SAT score for UCLA's admits?* somebody yelled out the answer every time. But when I asked, *Which college has its own golf course? Where can students water ski for free using the college's boats? Where did The Simpsons creator, Matt Groening, go to college?* nobody ever got those.

The Collegewise approach

There were plenty of college admissions counselors in the marketplace, but none approached it the way I saw it needed to be done. I knew if I could make the college admissions process enjoyable, it would resonate—and not just with the high achievers. I started Collegewise in 1999 and soon logged hundreds of miles driving to nine families' homes to work with students. I helped them choose colleges, fill out applications and brainstorm essays. The messages I carried with me were:

- Relax. It will be okay. You're going to enjoy this. Let's have some fun, people.

- I don't care what your GPA or your test scores are. If you want to go college and you're willing to do the work, let's get to it.

- We're not just going to focus on the 20 prestigious schools everyone else wants to attend. We're going to look around and find the right colleges for YOU, even if you haven't heard of them yet.

- You're not going spend hundreds of hours and unreasonable amounts of your parents' money in pursuit of higher SAT or ACT scores. You'll do some focused prep if you need to, take the test once or twice and then move on.

- I won't guide you to do particular activities just to pad your applications. Whether you play softball, do community service, cheerlead or work at an ice cream shop, I'll encourage you to keep doing it as long as you enjoy it.

- When you fill out college applications and write your essays, I won't try to package you, market you or do anything else that treats you like a widget capable of being reverse-engineered to impress colleges. I'll tell you to just be yourself.

- I won't do the work for you. You'll do your own college research, fill out the applications and write the essays. But like the smarter older brother who's gone through this before, I'll help you, give you advice and a little cheerleading, and relieve your parents from the project management details.

My phone started ringing. Within a year, I was working with more than 100 students.

Not an arms race

Some people see college planning as an escalating arms race where students must out-achieve, out-test and out-strategize the competition. They think the only acceptable outcome for their hard work is an offer of admission from a prestigious school. To them, this process isn't supposed to be fun, and stories like those of our Collegewise students' are anomalies.

I disagree. There's a better way to approach college admissions, and this book details the better way for you.

Collegewise has helped more than 5,000 kids—A students, C students and everyone in between—gain admission to more than 800 different colleges. Our students find schools where they can be happy and successful. They finish their applications months before their friends. They get accepted to schools they are excited to attend and receive generous—often unsolicited—financial aid and scholarships. When our students decide on their destination for the next four years, they buy sweatshirts bearing the names of their schools. Their parents slap decals on the family cars to announce their collegiate pride. They do more than just survive the college admissions process. They thrive—with less stress—and have fun along the way.

You can, too. I wrote the first version of this book to show you how.

What to expect

This is not a book about how to get into Harvard.

I start with same basic retraining–breaking down traditional college admissions notions that ruin the process for families. Then I show you how to find the right colleges for you. I reveal what colleges really look for from students, and teach you how to give it to them.

You'll learn the secrets to a successful and enjoyable high school career, tips to get better grades and test scores, and ways any student can impress teachers, counselors and colleges.

Every part of applying to college—the application, the essays and the interview—is covered. I also discuss how to pay for it with the help of financial aid and scholarships. There's even a section for your parents to suggest how they can support your search, but let you drive it.

If it's part of a successful, enjoyable ride to college, I cover it in this book.

My approach is a radical shift for some families, but it's not controversial or risky. Throughout this book, you'll hear from admissions professionals who echo my advice, and from former Collegewise students and parents who share how it worked for them.

This is college admissions the smarter, saner way.

Relax. It will be OK. You're going to enjoy this. Let's have some fun, people.

—Kevin McMullin
Founder and Head of Counseling
Collegewise
The Admissions Services Division of The Princeton Review

Basic Retraining:
How to Approach the College Admissions Process

I hate it, but I understand the frenzy. I have to understand it, because I watch the news, read the papers (and the books) that tell me that there is an education crisis. Except, I can't think of one student I know or have ever heard of who wanted to go to college, applied, and didn't get in anywhere. I've definitely heard students say that they didn't get into their 1st choice college, which can be frustrating, but not the end of the world. Furthermore, I don't know of a 'bad' college...There are some that might have nicer dorms, warmer climates, more access to professors, but it's all a matter of the student's taste. So what I'm saying is, there's good news. YOU ARE GOING TO COLLEGE. There. The pressure is off. Now the question is: where?

–Swarthmore College
Office of Admissions blog[1]

Basic Retraining
How to Approach the College Admissions Process

College Hopes and Worries

Every year in March, we release the results of our annual "College Hopes & Worries Survey," to coincide with what we call "the other March Madness": the nail-biting season from early march to mid-April as letters of college admissions decisions and financial aid packages land in family mailboxes.

We poll college applicants and their parents each year about their dream colleges and biggest worries, what they expect college to cost and how they expect to benefit from attending. The worries seem to grow bigger every year; last year more than two-thirds of roughly 14,000 respondents claimed their stress levels were "high" or "very high." More than a fifth of respondents year over year have reported they or their child plan to apply to nine or more schools. Last year more than a third of respondents reported that the toughest part of their experience was completing applications for admission and financial aid. And 87 percent said they expected the total cost of obtaining a degree would be more than $50,000, while 89 percent reported that financial aid would be "extremely" or "very" necessary.

There's no doubt about it: the college application process can be overwhelming, terrifying, downright decimating.

But only if you let it.

Applying to college shouldn't be this scary. It should be exciting—after all, this is the first step toward the rest of your life. If you're in the thick of prepping for your SATs and trying to make sense of the FAFSA, it's probably a challenge to feel excited, but trust us. We've spent our careers coaching nervous students and parents through standardized tests and college applications.

Focus on the good news

"Harvard, Princeton post record low acceptance rates"

CNNMoney ran this headline on March 30, 2012, right on cue.[2] Every spring, the major media outlets run features that suggest college admissions rates are dropping—again!

The doom and gloom headlines make the Collegewise phones ring. The high school students and their parents who call are so disillusioned about their college prospects. They hear that competition is fierce, that students have to be perfect to get in and that the kid who built a satellite got rejected from everywhere!

Here's the thing—the admissions squeeze is only true for a tiny percentage of colleges.

There are more than 2,000 four-year colleges and universities in this country, and the vast majority of them accept most of their applicants. In fall 2012, colleges reporting admissions data to The Princeton Review accepted, on average, 65 percent of their applicants, and 126 of those schools accepted 90 percent or higher. Whatever your GPA and test scores are, you can go to college if you really want to go. The only question is which one.

Contrary to what the media report, it's actually never been easier to get into college than it is today. A Stanford economics professor's 2009 study found that 90 percent of colleges are easier to get into today than they were in the 1950s and 1960s.[3] How can that be? Since 1955, the number of high school graduates has grown by 131 percent, but the number of college spots has raised 297 percent.[4] That's right—the number of available spots has outpaced the number of students vying for them.

Bottom line—there are more schools with more space for students than ever before.

Sure, Harvard, Columbia, Stanford, Yale and Princeton all accept less than 10 percent of their applicants. You could have perfect grades, perfect test scores and a certificate verifying that it was, in fact, you who invented plutonium. You still might not get into one of those schools. That's what happens when the highest-achieving applicants from all over the world apply to the same colleges. There are just too many applicants vying for a limited number of spaces.

How many colleges are highly selective?

We consider any college that accepts fewer than 20 percent of its applicants to be highly selective. We also consider these colleges the exception, not the norm. According to the data we collect annually from schools, only 40 colleges are actually that selective. Think Ivy League and Stanford. The list of colleges that accept 30 percent of their applicants is almost double that number, with 79 schools. Change the variable to 40 percent and it nearly doubles again to 151 schools. And a 50 percent acceptance rate yields 268 colleges.

That leaves more 1,600 schools that accept more than half their applicants.

You may not take solace in these statistics, but you're virtually guaranteed admission to hundreds of schools you haven't heard of (yet). We have a lot of ground to cover about how to find the right colleges for you and whether the most selective schools are among them.

Collegewise counselors and The Princeton Review's college guidebooks have helped thousands of students understand a fundamental truth about college admissions today: There's a school out there for you, probably one that will make you very happy. You just have to care enough about your future to want that for yourself and commit to doing the work to get there.

This book will show you how.

College Matchmaker

Visit The Princeton Review's college search online and see how many colleges there are to choose from: PrincetonReview.com

Myth: It's impossible for regular students to get in anymore

Impossible? Let's not get carried away. The trend toward hypercompetitive admissions often gets oversold in the news, because it disproportionately affects private East Coast universities. Admissions aren't nearly that restrictive at the vast majority of colleges.[5]

University of Wisconsin-Madison
Getting in: The not-so-secret admissions process

It's not that difficult

Remember that getting into a good college is not that difficult. It may not be a college that your grandmother has heard of, but you have a better choice of colleges and universities here than in any other country in the world. You might pause for a moment and appreciate that. Notice all those young people moving here from China, Korea, the Philippines, Egypt, Nigeria and other places? They know that you can get a splendid education in the United States with nothing more than a basic understanding of English and a willingness to work hard. The vast majority of colleges accept most of their applicants, and some good ones still have empty spaces in September.[6]

Jay Mathews
Washington Post

Worry less about college

When families arrive at Collegewise or pick up our *Best Colleges* guide for the first time, many of them are stressed and overwhelmed. The students worry about finding a school that will accept them with their 2.8 GPA or that their perfect credentials won't be good enough for a prestigious college. They're scared of making a mistake, and they're not having much fun with college planning. That's why the first piece of advice we almost always give to them is simple—relax.

You live in the country that has the most coveted and accessible system of higher education in the world. About six out of every ten students who graduated from high school in 2012 enrolled in four-year colleges or universities.[7] Almost two-thirds of high school graduates who apply to college get in. You're almost certainly going to college no matter what your GPA or SAT score. Wherever you go, it'll be an intellectual supermarket where you can learn, explore, discover, meet people and have fun for four years. You, not the name of your college, will get to determine just how successful you are after graduation.

A student's college future is serious business. But that doesn't mean the process of finding and applying to college can't be an exciting time that families can enjoy together. Have enough confidence in yourself to know you're going to work hard and be successful wherever you go. You'll enjoy high school a lot more, and you'll be more successful getting into college.

Worrying constantly about whether your SAT scores are good enough for Yale, or how many APs it takes to get into Duke, or what Stanford wants you to say in your essays just make you focus on the wrong things.

More than 5,000 students have come through the Collegewise offices and just about all of them ended up with college options they were excited about. College admissions tip No. 1: Relax.

Work hard. Worry less. It's all going to be okay.

Put yourself in charge

You're the one who's going to college—not your parents or your high school counselor. You shouldn't expect anybody else to do the work for you. The more you take charge of your college future, the more successful you're going to be.

It's your job to care enough about your future to research colleges. It's your job to fill out your applications and write your essays. It's your job to make sure you meet all your deadlines and follow up with the colleges to make sure they've received your materials. If these things aren't taken care of, it's not going to affect anyone more than it affects you. That's why you need to be in charge.

We're not saying you have to do all of this alone. You should absolutely ask for advice from people you trust. Your parents and your counselor, in particular, should be on your support team. They can answer questions, cheer you on, help you make good decisions and even review your work. But don't let them do the work for you. Don't wait for them to research college application requirements, fill out your applications, or call the admissions offices to ask questions for you. Those are your jobs, not theirs. Your college future is too important for you to be a passive bystander.

The more you do for yourself during the college admissions process, the more successful that process is going to be. You'll find colleges that fit you rather than having them chosen for you. You'll have better answers when those colleges' applications and interviewers ask you why you've decided to apply to their schools. And most importantly, you'll get accepted to more colleges that you're excited about.

Once you get to college, nobody's going to run your life for you. So this is the time to show colleges, your parents, and yourself that you're mature enough to take charge of your own future.

Work, work, work hard

While we do spend a lot of time at Collegewise offices and Princeton Review events telling our students to relax, we have never once told a student that it's okay not to work hard.

Effort is the great equalizer. Your success in life will have much more to do with the amount of effort you put in day-to-day than your GPA, SAT score or whether or not you went to a famous college. We tell our students that once they put out an effort they can be proud of, they earn the right to relax and have faith that everything will be okay.

Behind most success stories, you'll usually find a tale of hard work. The Beatles were just a struggling high school band in 1960 when they were first invited to play in Hamburg, Germany. By the time they hit it big four years later, they'd performed live approximately 1,200 times, sometimes for as long as eight hours a night. Most bands today don't perform 1,200 times in their entire careers. The Beatles weren't The Beatles until they worked hard enough to earn it.[8]

When he was growing up, writer and actor Seth Rogen (from *This is the End*, *Superbad*, and *Pineapple Express*) worked hard at being funny. When he was 12, he signed up for a stand-up comedy class. When he was 13, he and a friend wrote the original screenplay for Superbad which, years later, became a major motion picture. By the time he got to high school, people were paying him to do stand-up comedy at bar mitzvahs, parties and bars. When he was 16, he won the Vancouver Amateur Comedy Contest.[9] He wasn't just the funny guy at school. He took classes to learn how to be funny, worked jobs to practice his comedy and even entered contests to see how he stacked up against other comedians. That's a lot of effort.

If you take challenging classes and put in the effort, it doesn't matter if your GPA isn't perfect. You'll be smarter and even better prepared for college because of your effort.

If you've spent every Saturday of the last two years volunteering in a program that helps elementary school kids at inner city schools with their homework, does it really matter in the grand scheme of things whether Cornell says, "Yes"?

You've worked hard, you've helped people and you deserve to be proud of that. College admissions officers will notice, too.

Lack of effort holds you back

Just like hard work will always take you someplace, a lack of effort eventually catches up with you. If you refuse to work hard and get by with C's through high school and college, the kids who go to Harvard are going to have huge advantages over you after graduation. But it won't be because they went to Harvard and you went to a less famous school. It will be because they worked much harder than you did.

Even the most successful people were never great at everything they tried. But just about all of them worked hard to get where they are. When he was 27, Mark Cuban, the current owner of the Dallas Mavericks basketball team, got fired from his job as a computer salesman. So he started a software reseller and system integration company called MicroSolutions out of his apartment and stayed up late every night learning as much as he could about new software. Seven years later, he sold MicroSolutions for $6 million.[10] Not a bad turnaround.

We all have natural strengths and weaknesses. We can't all get perfect grades, be award-winning musicians or make it in Hollywood. But YOU get to decide how hard you're willing to work. Putting in the effort will always take you to good places.

Think about the big picture

Many kids prepare for college by focusing only on short-term gains. They take an extra AP class because that will boost their GPA. They volunteer at the homeless shelter because they want more community service hours. They visit a teacher after class to ask how to get extra credit so they can get an A. They're preparing for college like mercenaries—everything they do is based on short-term advantages they think can help them get what they want. That's like getting married so you can combine two incomes to buy a nicer car. Mercenaries miss the bigger picture.

Just about everything you do to prepare for college has bigger life implications, too.

- When you work hard in your classes in high school, you become smarter and better educated.

- When you find and commit yourself to activities you enjoy, you discover your talents, learn to work with other people and enjoy life outside of the classroom.

- When you learn how to do things for yourself without relying on your parents, you become more independent and better prepared to live on your own.

- When you find a subject that interests you and dive in to learn more, you see for yourself just how rewarding learning can be when you let your interests take you there.

- When you struggle in a class and approach your teacher for help, you learn how to advocate for yourself and how to seek out assistance when you need it.

- When you try your best and still come up short, you learn how to handle that failure or disappointment and then move on.

- When you take all those lessons with you to college, you get more out of the experience.

As you go through high school and plan for college, don't just focus on what admissions advantage you're getting. Think about the life advantages, too. There's no guarantee anything you do will get you into one particular school. But everything you do gives you a bigger life advantage. Those bigger advantages guarantee that you'll get in someplace and that you'll also be more successful once you get there.

It's not just about getting in

...scheduling every minute of your life in order to get into college is nutty; and most importantly, it's a dumb way to live your life. If you're doing all that stuff because you love it, have a passion for it, and/or can't bear to live without it, fine by me. Trying to join every single activity that MIGHT give you some miniscule assistance in some mythical admissions process, however, is deeply misguided.[11]

Andrew Flagel
Dean of Admissions
George Mason University

Be a kid

Your high school career should be about lots of things, and preparing for college is certainly one of them. But a lot of high school students are so stressed about college that they're not enjoying their lives. You need to have a little fun, too.

In 2013, The Princeton Review surveyed more than 14,000 college applicants and their parents. Sixty-nine percent of them said their stress levels were "high" or "very high" (up 15 percent from 2003, the survey's initial year). Studies by the University of Kentucky found seniors in high school average less than seven hours of sleep a night, and only 5 percent of high school seniors average eight hours.[12] That kind of overstressed, overworked and overscheduled lifestyle is hazardous to your mental health, as well as to your college admissions chances.

You can't produce great work constantly. Your brain and your body need time off when you're not being measured and evaluated. So read the occasional gossip mag. Listen to music. Play video games. Throw a Frisbee. Throw water balloons at your siblings. Teach yourself to play guitar. Sketch. Write poetry. Watch bad television every now and then. Spend time daydreaming, exploring and exposing yourself to things that seem fun or interesting. Goof off with your friends. Be a kid for crying out loud.

Think you're too busy for the luxury of downtime? Consider this: Berkshire Hathaway CEO Warren Buffett, one of the richest people in the world, plays a mean ukulele and gives lessons to a girls' club in Omaha, Neb.[13] Former Secretary of State and First Lady Hilary Clinton does crossword puzzles.[14] And almost all of 166 Nobel laureates in chemistry have had an enduring hobby, from chess to insect collecting.[15] If they can find downtime and enjoy things just for fun, you can, too.

A former Collegewise student wrote his entire college essay about how much he liked to sing country music in the shower. He said he actually looked forward to doing it every day after baseball practice. His mother would knock on the door and yell, "Honey, are you having a rock concert in there?!" It was his time to do something that had absolutely nothing to do with getting into college, and he enjoyed every second of it. He also got accepted to his first-choice college, University of San Diego.

Yes, colleges want students who know how to work hard. That's why they accept students who've taken challenging curriculums, done well, and made some substantial commitments to outside activities. They also want students who are happy and well-adjusted kids who know how to enjoy their lives.

Create your own magic formula

Some students spend their high school years searching for the magic formula for admission to their dream college. The logic is that if they combine the right mix of classes, test scores and activities, say the right things in their essays, talk to the right people and apply under the right major, they'll be a sure thing. Their high school years become a complex game of strategy in the hopes of gaming the system and getting into their dream schools.

In fact, a magic formula for college admissions doesn't exist. If it did, someone would have discovered and profited from it already.

There's nothing wrong with being goal oriented. But trying to reverse engineer yourself to please particular colleges won't work. Making every decision in high school—from what classes to take, to which activities to do, to what to write in your college essays—based on what you think will impress your dream colleges is a terrible way to stand out. And it's certainly no way to make you happy.

College admission is a personal, often subjective process. It might seem unfair that your favorite colleges won't just tell you exactly what to do to get admitted. But this is the way the world works, too. There's no magic formula for getting a job at Google, either. Learning the right skills, working hard and getting good experience will improve anyone's chances of eventually getting to work at the Googleplex. But there's still no itemized checklist to follow.

Work hard. Do what you love. Select appropriate colleges and present yourself honestly. That's the only college admissions strategy that works.

COMMITTEE NOTES

There is no formula

Trying to define admissions with a formula is like trying to define life with a formula. It's like trying to explain poetry using calculus. It would take the human component out of it, which is perhaps the most important part.[16]

Ben Jones
Former Director of Communication
Office of Admissions
MIT

It is not a game to be played

The application process is not a "reward" for the hard work you've put in during high school. (The rewards are the grades you've earned and, ultimately, the education you've acquired.) It is not a game to be played, and for all the strategizing people think works, the gaming approach is one that is fairly obvious to us and doesn't usually yield a positive result.[17]

Swarthmore College
Office of Admissions blog

Think more what than where

Going to college is important. It's a life-changing experience that's worth just about any reasonable sacrifice you and your parents can make so you can go. The difference between life with a college degree and life without one is huge. (In 2011, the median earnings for bachelor's degree recipients working full-time were $21,100 higher than those of high school graduates.[18]) That said, the name of the school on the degree won't be nearly as important as what you do while you're there.

You can passively go through your college years, study enough to get by and have a little fun. Or you can take advantage of the fact that you have four years of virtually unlimited opportunities to learn whatever you want to learn, discover your real talents, find mentors, build work experience and have *a lot* of fun.

Case in point: a former Collegewise student—a male—went to the University of Arizona where he tried out and made the practice squad of their NCAA Division I women's basketball team. The coach saw advantages to having her starters practice against players who were bigger and stronger. So the team held open tryouts for guys who'd played basketball in high school. Our student got full athletic privileges, including priority registration and free tutoring. When he graduated and started applying for jobs, he told us that every single interview he went on asked him about playing women's basketball. He was gainfully employed in marketing for a major league baseball team less than three weeks after graduating from college.

Other former Collegewise students have worked with a professor to find an AIDS vaccine, built a working submarine with other mechanical engineering majors, worked as a resident advisor and spent an evening counseling a student who was considering suicide, and tripled the fundraising revenue as a volunteer at a non-profit. All were significant life experiences. Not all of these happened at "prestigious" colleges.

Every college will give you opportunities to learn, explore your passions, develop your talents and create a remarkable experience for yourself. It will be up to you to take advantage of the opportunities and extract the value your college has to offer, whether it's atop all the college ranking lists or some tiny school your friends have never heard of.

The key is finding a college that's right for you—one with an environment where you can really be happy and successful. 🎓

Finding Fits:

How to Find
the Right Colleges for You

" *Instead of sticking to colleges* that I already knew about, my Collegewise counselor encouraged me to research a large number of different kinds of colleges. Some I had never even heard of before. When I was doing the research, I figured out what I was really looking for in a college, and what I didn't like about some colleges. My counselor would not accept BS answers, even though at first I tried to give some. She pushed me to really consider what I liked and disliked about each college. I received acceptances from 11 universities and 9 offered me academic scholarships. I committed to SMU and accepted their Provost Scholarship award. If not for my college research, I would never have known about SMU. **"**

Aaron F.
Former Collegewise student, Class of 2012
Southern Methodist University

Do Finding Fits:
How to Find the Right Colleges for You

How to cure namebranditis

Beware of popular opinions

Trying to convince some people that Harvard isn't necessarily better than a less famous school is like trying to convince the guy sleeping in line outside the Apple Store that the iPhone isn't a better product than a Blackberry. No matter how much evidence you show them to the contrary, some people just won't be convinced. That's fine—they have the right to keep seeing the world the way they see it. If that sounds like you (about the colleges, not the phones), let's just agree to disagree.

The students Collegewise works with who get into Ivy League schools, paradoxically, tend to be less enamored with the schools' prestige and more enamored with the opportunities for learning. As soon as we hear a kid say, "I want to go to an Ivy League school," it's almost a certainty that he just won't have the intellectual curiosity to get there. He's in love with the image, not with the learning.

Students convinced that prestigious colleges are the best colleges are also the ones who spend high school trying to please a short list of dream schools that will most likely reject them. Then they are absolutely crushed if those schools say no. That's giving an awful lot of power to just a few colleges.

Good kids who work hard deserve better than that.

Just to get them out of the way, here are our responses to a few biases we hear every now and then from people suffering from namebranditis (our term for the affliction that causes sufferers to fall overly in love with only prestigious, name-brand schools).

"C'mon. How can you say that prestigious colleges aren't great schools?"

We're not saying they aren't great schools. We're saying their prestige doesn't make them *better* schools.

You can get a fabulous education at Princeton, Stanford, Harvard, Duke, University of Chicago, UC Berkeley or any other highly selective college. All of them will surround you with opportunities to learn, grow, and meet intellectual, driven, interesting students. We've worked with students who went on to these schools and were blissfully happy. There's no scam there.

But so much of the pressure about getting into college today comes from the belief that prestigious colleges who reject almost everyone are somehow better schools; that people who get into prestigious colleges are destined for success and those who get rejected are starting life deep in the end zone. There's very little evidence to support such a belief.

The University of Iowa's Ernest Pascarella coauthored How College Affects Students, an 827-page analysis of hundreds of studies on how various colleges affect students, including intellectual growth, moral development, career advancement and economic impacts. "We haven't found any convincing evidence that selectivity or prestige matters," Pascarella said.[1]

Another study by Pascarella and George Kuh of Indiana University showed that selective schools don't systematically employ better educational practices than less selective schools do. In fact, in three areas—the number of essay examinations given, instructor feedback to students and having a supportive campus environment—selective schools actually scored worse.[2]

There are at least 100 other colleges whose offerings are indistinguishable from those at the prestigious colleges. You can get the same education and opportunities from less-selective schools. It's just going to be up to you to put the work in to benefit from your time there. What you do in college is more important than where you go.

"I've worked really hard in high school. Why should I settle for a less-selective college?"

If you've worked really hard in high school, the last thing you should do is settle. We're not saying you should lower your standards. We're saying there are more schools out there that meet your standards than you may think.

You should go to a college you're excited about. You should go to a college where you'll be surrounded by other students who care enough about their future to have worked as hard as you have. You should go someplace where you can meet people, have fun, find what you're good at and get a little smarter every day. You deserve those things, and good news: more than only 40 schools in the country can give them to you.

Yes, there are vast differences between the colleges that accept almost nobody and those that accept almost everybody. We understand most high-achieving students wouldn't be happy attending a college full of underachievers. But you've got to go pretty deep down the list of more than 2,000 U.S. colleges before those differences become noticeable, deeper than 30 or 80 or even 100. Just because a school isn't as prestigious as an Ivy League school doesn't mean it's full of substandard students.

Applying to a short list of prestigious schools and then just hoping one will take you puts your college destiny up to a short list of prestigious colleges. You've worked too hard for that.

"Most people who graduate from prestigious colleges seem very impressive."

Maybe so, but is that because they went to prestigious schools? Our bet is they worked hard to become impressive before they ever went to college.

Harvard received a record 34,303 applications for the Class of 2017. Among the applicants, 95 percent were ranked in the top 10 percent of their high school senior class. Harvard only has about 2,000 spaces in its freshman class. There's no way around that math. Most of those applicants were rejected.

Will anybody be surprised if those 2,000 Harvard freshmen eventually go on to do great things in their lives? Of course not. No one is saying Harvard won't give them a great education. But Harvard isn't putting lipstick on a pig. Those students' future successes were born from qualities they developed long before they ever took up residence near Harvard Yard. We're talking about their work ethic, interest in learning, character, persistence, and maybe even their personality and charm.

What about the 32,300 amazingly brilliant and accomplished applicants Harvard rejected for the Class of 2017? Are they doomed to substandard lives now that they won't have Harvard degrees? We don't think so. They're too brilliant and accomplished to be left behind.

Smart, hard-working, passionate kids will almost certainly make something of themselves wherever they go.

"You can't beat the connections you get from going to a prestigious college."

It's not like the prestigious colleges give you an all-access membership card to a club that hires for all the great jobs. Valuable connections are a product of doing the difficult work to earn them, not by attending a school with a famous name.

Lots of less-famous schools will give you the opportunities to learn from great professors, meet mentors, get involved, discover your passions, and work hard enough to impress people who will help you take your next step after graduation. It's going to be up to you to earn those connections, whether or not you're at a famous school.

Do a success search

Here's a good way to learn more about just how many colleges, famous and not-so-famous, can lead to success. Ask successful adults in your life where they went to college.

Pick five adults you know and respect that are doing something you find interesting—your family doctor, your boss at your internship, your dad's business partner, etc. Ask them where they went to college and what they majored in. If you don't want to ask them, Google them. Either way, connect the dots from where they started and where they are now.

You'll likley find there isn't a lot of correlation between how successful they are and the relative prestige of their colleges. Some of them may have gone to prestigious schools, but a lot of them won't have. Like most successful people, they probably got where they are today by working hard and making the most of opportunities that presented themselves along the way. These conversations can also lead to some interesting revelations about college, what they got out of their experiences, and the roles their schools played in getting them where they are. Case in point: a dad and his daughter were leaving a Collegewise office once and he saw a Grinnell College pennant on the wall. He said, "That place changed my life. I wouldn't be where I am today if I hadn't gone there."

Grinnell is a small liberal arts college in the middle of rural Iowa. The school has a good sense of humor about their location and their lack of Ivy League prestige—they sell T-shirts in the school bookstore that read, "Where the hell is Grinnell?" on the front, and "Who the hell cares?" on the back.

The Collegewise dad is a neurosurgeon.

Look outside the family circle

If you're not convinced by your immediate circles that a degree from a prestigious college is not a prerequisite for success, take the time to look up some famously successful people. Take 30 minutes at the computer and do a success search.

Would you say that someone who gets into Harvard Law School is on a pretty successful track? According to the school's website, the students enrolled in Harvard Law's Class of 2013 came from 261 undergraduate institutions, including dozens of not-so-name-brand colleges (e.g., Adelphi, Cal State Northridge, and Mary Washington).[4]

Consider the twelve Nobel Prize winners in 2013. Four went to prestigious colleges. Five went to less-famous schools. And three attended colleges with virtually no name recognition in the United States.

You can test this theory yourself. Look up where the governor of your state or the mayor of your town went to college. Pick a company whose products you like and find out where their leadership went to college. Type the name of your hero into Google and see what you find.

Try, for example, searching for "President of the American Medical Association," a position most everybody would agree connotes success. The current president, Ardis Dee Hoven, MD, received both her undergraduate degree in microbiology and her medical degree from the University of Kentucky, Lexington.

Some of the happy and successful people in the world went to Ivy League colleges, but there are many, many more that did not.

Sometimes kids know best

When our daughter began examining her college options, we thought she should apply to our alma mater and schools with highly recognizable names—it was the best assurance of employment upon graduation. She shocked us when she told us her favorite school was one of which we had never heard. It possessed a liberal arts emphasis and was clear across the country. We dismissed it, thinking there was no way she'd go there. Well, she is completing her sophomore year at that college and loves it. She completed an internship in Spain last summer and is looking forward to a summer of classical studies in Greece this year, one typically attended by grad students. She has grown in ways we would have never imagined. She is making an impact, following her own path, not ours, but a promising one just the same. Sometimes our kids do know best. It's their life and there's a point at which you have to trust and support their decisions.

Carol S.
Mother of Becca, former Collegewise student, Class of 2010
St. John's College (MD)

Have swagger—it'll serve you

The prognosis for a bad case of namebranditis is not good. You're less likely to enjoy the high school years. You'll be stressed throughout the college admissions process. Worst of all, you probably won't get into those prestigious schools you want to go to so badly.

People who get into highly selective colleges don't worship at the altar of prestige. They have too much confidence for that. They know they're going to be successful wherever they go. That confidence and immunity to namebranditis lets them find the right schools for them.

Getting into college is a lot like dating. Confidence is contagious. A little swagger is good.

The kid that worries that his life will be over if Princeton says, "No"—guess what? No swagger there.

7. What would you like to do on a typical Tuesday night in college? What about on a typical Saturday night?

This is a fun question because it's not necessarily the same as "What activities do you want to do in college?" The answers to this one draw out everything from the types of students you want to be around to where the campus is located to what you want to major in.

When we ask our Collegewise students, we get answers like, "Playing video games with my new friends in the dorms," "Talking politics in the coffee shop," "Heading into the city to do something fun," "Building a working robot with the other engineers," and "Going to the big football game."

This question also gets at just how comfortable you are with the idea of students drinking and doing other things they may not tell their parents about. With some notable exceptions, like the military academies and strict religious affiliated colleges, a certain percentage of kids at every school are going to find a way to have their good ol' college fun. Just how prevalent do you want that kind of fun to be?

You're only in class for a couple hours a day at most in college. The rest of the time, you're living your life on (or off) campus with your fellow students. Think about what you'd like to be doing in your free time and look for where that will be possible (See "50 Things You Can Do in College" on page TK if you need help brainstorming).

8. Do you want to go to college in a place that's different or similar to where you live now?

This one hits on everything from your city and state, to the size of your town, to the type of people in your community. College can be a four-year opportunity to live in a different place very different from where you live now. But that's not the right opportunity for everyone. It's good to consider just how much change you want to take on when you go to college.

One former Collegewise student said he wanted to be someplace very different because, "I've lived in the same gated community my entire life and gone to school with the same group of kids since I was five."

When he later applied to college, he mentioned that need for change in a lot of his "Why do you want to attend this college?" essays. One of those essays began, "I have never met anyone from Arkansas, and I think it's about time that I do."

Talking politics

Weekend afternoons are spent doing homework or sitting in my friends' rooms listening to blues and jazz stations as we sip black coffee over political discussions.

Alex H.
Former Collegewise student, Class of 2010
American University

Hitting the town

Life at the University of Denver is always lively; there's a ton of activities to do on the weekends right on campus, including things like movie nights and just finding different things people are doing in their dorms...there's always something going on. Still, if you're looking for more to do, you can head downtown with the light rail which is right across the street from the north side of campus. I'm practically never bored here.

Matt P.
Former Collegewise student, Class of 2011
University of Denver

Going natural

I spend my weekends hiking through the forest with friends, climbing an 80-foot tree, exploring the caves on campus, going down the Hobbit Hole, swinging on tree swings, camping in the forts built by students, swimming in the Garden of Eden and seeing AMAZING concerts at The Catalyst (Rebelution, Jenny Lewis, Matisyahu, Mason Jennings!). If you're someone who is down for adventures, loves nature, would attend drum circles on the full moon, cares about what's happening in the world, and is ready for a good time that doesn't involve theme parties...then Santa Cruz is the place for you.

Anne Marie S.
Former Collegewise student, Class of 2008
UC Santa Cruz

Have fun visiting

For many high school students and parents, the idea of visiting colleges feels more like a homework assignment than it does an adventure. They feel pressure to visit ALL the colleges they're interested in, to turn every visit into an intense fact-finding mission, and to do all of it while the colleges are in session as opposed to over the summer. Those expectations can make college visits stressful and not nearly as fun as they should be. So here are some visit tips to help you enjoy what should be a positive part of the college search process.

1. No need to visit all your chosen schools before applying.

"Visit all your schools before you apply," is great advice in theory. But it's just not practical, especially if you're applying to colleges far away (and in many different directions from your home). Remember that you can also visit colleges after you apply, and even after you get accepted.

GO TO THE SOURCE, TOO

As you narrow your college list, make sure you visit the websites of the schools that interest you. Read about their admissions requirements and the academic profiles of students they admit. Good books and website tools are helpful in finding potential college fits. But they're not a replacement for the information each college publishes on its site.

You apply to most colleges in the fall of your senior year. You hear back around March, and you usually have until May 1 of your senior year to make a decision. That means there are five to seven months after you apply when you can still visit colleges.

Before you apply, gravitate toward schools near places you're visiting anyway, like for a sports tournament, a band competition or even a Thanksgiving weekend at Uncle Frank's house. That will get you the most bang for your visit buck.

Also, prioritize visiting schools you aren't yet convinced of. This gives you the chance to fall in love or decide they're not right for you. The rest, you can save until after you apply.

2. Don't limit your visits to "reach" schools.

Many students plan visits to only their top choices, which all too often are schools most likely to reject them. Instead of widening their college choices by visiting schools where their chances of admission are solid, they're narrowing the pool by renewing vows to dream schools.

If you love Duke, if you've cheered on their basketball team since you were 12 years old and simply cannot envision a universe where you wouldn't apply to Duke, you don't need to fall any deeper in love with Duke by visiting the campus. Spend this time visiting other colleges, preferably some more likely to love you back. Baylor, Gonzaga, Syracuse and Michigan State have great basketball teams, rabid fans, and a lot less competition for spots in the freshman class. If your Duke admission comes through in the spring, then go see the home of the Blue Devils.

3. A summer visit is better than no visit.

Some students are told to only visit a college when it is in session; that visiting over the summer doesn't give you the same feel as when the campus teems with students. There's some truth to it—a lot of colleges are deserted over the summer and it's absolutely not the same as it is in the fall. But it's not easy to put your high school classes and activities on hold to go see colleges, so the visit-while-it's-in-session logic doesn't always hold up.

If you can visit a college during the school year, do it, especially if you want to sit in on a class, get a sense of whether a big school's population is too much for you or do anything else that only is revealed when students are there. But if you just want to see the campus or find out just how small the college's small town really is, a summer visit is probably fine, and certainly better than not visiting at all. Before you make the trek, just check the college's website to make sure they'll be offering tours while you're there.

4. Don't see more colleges in one trip than you can handle.

It's possible to commit college-visit overkill by trying to see too many colleges in one trip. One former Collegewise student only somewhat sarcastically recalled her family's marathon college tour: "We saw four colleges the first day, another four the second day, and I was like, 'I don't want to go to college anymore—I just want to go home,'" she said.

We understand why this happens to families. If you're going to take the time to travel someplace to see colleges, it makes sense that you should see as many as possible as long as you're there. But the average person wouldn't enjoy seeing nine

Deciding which colleges to actually apply to is one of the most important decisions you make in college planning. And while there are many people who can give you good advice about what colleges you might like, one of the best sources of advice about your chances of admission is your high school counselor.

Your high school counselor doesn't just know you—she knows college admissions. She knows which students from your school have been admitted to which colleges in the past. She knows how you stack up against those students. That's not information you can get from friends, a college guidebook or even the colleges themselves.

So make an appointment with your high school counselor and show her your list. Ask her what she thinks your chances of admission are, and give her permission to be honest. Listen to what she has to say, even if you don't like the answers.

It's fine to ask for clarification so you can better understand. But you are not allowed to get all torqued up if every school on your list only accepts fifteen out of every hundred students who apply, and your counselor says your odds of admission are slim.

The best time to visit your counselor and get approval? May of your junior year, not the fall of your senior year, for three reasons:

1. Counselors are at their busiest during the fall. It's a new school year, students are still getting their schedules adjusted and the seniors are coming in with all their requests for college application support.

2. If your list is out of whack, you'll have the summer to do more research and find appropriate replacements.

3. If your list is approved (or mostly approved), you can start on your applications and essays over the summer.

Additional advantages

There are some additional advantages to getting your counselor's approval of your list. If you're eventually deferred or wait-listed, your counselor may be able to call the school and find out information about your chances of being admitted in the next round. But you're a lot more likely to have your counselor on your support team if she approved the list in the first place.

Bottom line: make sure you have a balanced college list of target schools. It's fine to have a few schools that are out of your admissions reach, but the best way to end up with choices you're happy with is to apply where your chances of admission are strong.

Don't get that advice from friends, hearsay or any other source. Your counselor is a great source for that information, and your college list is too important not to ask the question.

Love your list

Admissions uncertainty makes a lot of applicants apply to schools they're not that excited about. They just feel better knowing they have a lot of applications out there. You're probably not going to love every college on your list equally, but it's good to be in full-blown like with every school on your list. Don't apply to any school just to see what happens.

If you'd rather go to juvenile hall than actually attend one of your safeties, why bother applying? Focus your safety schools on those you'd actually be excited to attend. If you can't find safety schools you like, you've probably got namebranditis, not a lack of good options.

If you apply to all the Ivy League schools just because they're prestigious, you don't really like those schools. You like the *idea* of those schools.

If you load up your college list with lots of options that you haven't researched because you're afraid you won't get into enough schools, relax and trim the fat off your list. Applying to schools you're not really interested in just makes more work for you and takes time away from your applications to schools that mean more to you. If you've done your college soul searching and had your counselor approve your list, you'll be fine. 🎓

COMMITTEE NOTES

Fall in list love

Here is my advice: Love your list. In the landscape of higher education, there is no excuse for feeling "bleh" about a school you apply to. Honestly, if you can't see yourself going there, why spend the effort writing essays, filling out forms, and shelling out application fees? Love your list. Pick schools that deserve your talents but do not abandon reality. 'Safety school,' 'match school,' and 'reach school' should still be phrases running through your head. However, should loving your safety school be a foreign idea? Imagine getting that first acceptance letter and genuinely being thrilled...whoa...[11]

Justin Pike

The better your academic performance, the more college options you will have. Challenging yourself sanely means that you enroll in the most difficult classes you can handle. Don't lock yourself into a curriculum that ruins high school for you. If you already have, talk to your parents and your counselor about making some changes so you can start challenging yourself sanely.

Ask for a drop option

At most colleges, students can jump in and try a course for a couple weeks to see if they like it. If they don't want to take the course for any reason, they can drop it. As long as they do so within a specified trial period, there are no negative impacts on their academic records. Savvy high school students find out if their schools will let them do the same.

Some high schools have a stated policy about how long you can stay in a particular course before you drop it. Other schools leave it up to counselors to decide on a case-by-case basis. No matter where you go to high school: (1) know what the policy is, and (2) ask about the option before you begin a course—not out of necessity after you get a D-plus on your first exam.

When you ask your counselor, make it clear you're asking because you want to take an academic risk and challenge yourself, not because you want an escape hatch if you blow it and don't study for your tests. For example, if you're picking classes for next year and you're unsure about AP Chemistry because you tend to struggle in your science courses, tell your counselor about your concern. Let her know you really want to try the course, but you're wondering if you'd be allowed to drop it if AP Chem got the best of you. The drop option should encourage you to embrace a challenge.

If your counselor gives you parameters in which you could drop the course, jump in and do everything you can to not exercise that option.

Even if your counselor tells you there isn't a drop option, you'll establish yourself as a student who's academically self-aware enough to anticipate challenges and mature enough to discuss them.

Embrace a challenge

It's usually easier to drop down from a more-rigorous track to a less-rigorous one; so if you're on the fence, challenge yourself with a more-rigorous load, and drop down if it ends up being too difficult to handle. We love students who embrace a challenge.[5]

Swarthmore College
Office of Admissions blog

Follow your favorite subjects

When planning a course of study with a counselor at Collegewise, students often ask questions like:

"Which one: AP U.S. History or AP Chemistry?"
"Should I take a fourth year of language?"
"Can I take AP Psychology instead of AP Calculus?"

When you have questions like that, here's a good place to start: ask yourself where your interest overlaps with the biggest challenge.

If you don't want to take both AP US History and AP Chemistry simultaneously, pick the one that looks more interesting to you, dive in and learn as much as you can.

If you're not sure whether to take a fourth year of language, ask yourself how much language really interests you. If you're a lot happier learning math than you are Spanish, or if your geometry teacher was one of the best teachers you've ever had and she also teaches calculus, consider trading Spanish and taking calculus.

If you want to take AP Psychology instead of AP Calculus, be honest about why you want to do that. If it's because AP Psychology just isn't as hard as AP Calculus and you still want the extra grade point from an AP class, you're not exerting the effort or following an interest.

Admissions officers want to see flashes of your academic interests. College interviewers routinely ask about your favorite subjects and teachers. The students who've thought about their favorite subjects and worked especially hard in them always have the best answers to those questions.

COMMITTEE NOTES

When challenges meet interests

My take: first, you should try picking courses because they interest and challenge you, and not just to get into a school, since there are plenty of schools and just maybe you should focus on the best learning for yourself. The Collegeboard seems to want EVERY student to take AS MANY AP COURSES AS POSSIBLE. I think that leads to a bit of insanity, and maybe a complete lack of a life. I do think, however, that it's great to challenge yourself when given the opportunity and the interest. I've mentioned before that one thing to consider is how much you think a course might drop your grades. If it's going from an A- to a B+, I wouldn't sweat it. If you're pretty sure taking the AP is going to drop from a solid B to a low C or even risk a D, I think that may be a bad decision.[6]

Andrew Flagel
Dean of Admissions and Associate Vice President
for Enrollment Development
George Mason University

How to get better grades (and study less)

Make class time study time

You know that kid who says he barely studied for a test and still gets an A? One way he does it: he makes the most of class time.

Imagine you knew at the conclusion of every class there would be an immediate test on the material. What would you do differently? You'd really pay attention. You'd try to soak up every piece of information and commit it to memory. If something wasn't clear, you'd ask a question. And you'd look for cues from your teacher about what material will be tested—cues including:

- Anything the teacher writes on the board.

- Anything the teacher repeats, makes a big deal of or emphasizes in any way (sounds like, "This was a crucial turning point for the United States in World War II.").

- Anything your teacher discusses at great length (if you're studying the Great Depression all week but spend two days on the reasons for the stock market crash, that's a tip).

- If your teacher goes to the trouble to make a handout.

- If your teacher spends a lot of time talking about something that isn't mentioned anywhere in the textbook.

The in-class study time adds up fast. Let's say your math teacher gives a test every three weeks. If you're in that class for one hour a day, five days a week and you treat it like study time, you'll already have studied 15 hours by the time your test arrives.

How much additional studying will you need to do? Not much. You'll be that kid who studies just a little bit for the test and still does well.

Start before you need to

If you start studying for a biology test before you need to, you'll find the concepts you're still not sure about and be able to visit your teacher after class to clear them up before the test.

If you start writing your essay for English class before you need to, you can ask your teacher to read a rough draft, and you can incorporate her feedback.

If you start your history project before you need to, you'll have more time to research it and put it together. You'll be able be able to practice your delivery and get to sleep earlier the night before.

Starting late lets the deadline decide when and how you spend your time. Starting early puts you in charge. You get to decide when to start and how much time to spend. You can work in short, focused bursts instead of one frantic marathon. You won't have to miss out on fun activities with your friends because you have a project due in two days.

Don't cop out and say that you work best under pressure. The president's speechwriter doesn't wait to start writing the State of the Union until even the week before it's presented. Great work takes time to produce. The first step is to have the discipline to start something before you need to.

Eliminate study-time interruptions

If you're answering emails, texting or checking Facebook every five minutes while trying to study, you're going to spend a lot more time than you need to get your work done.

Students age 8 to 18 today use entertainment media almost eight hours a day.[7] That's almost as many hours a day as the typical adult spends working a full-time job, and it can have consequences.

Driving while using a cell phone reduces the amount of brain activity associated with driving by 37 percent.[8] Text messaging creates a crash risk 23 times worse than driving while not distracted.[9] Nobody's going to get hurt because you text while doing your history homework. But if using your cell phone makes it harder to drive safely, it probably also affects your ability to solve chemistry equations.

Next time you sit down to do your homework and study, eliminate all your potential electronic distractions. Turn off your phone and shut down your computer. If you need your computer to do the work, close your email and instant messaging, and log out of Facebook.

If your house is bustling with activity and you can't concentrate, find a quiet place where you won't be disturbed, like a library. Then take note of how much faster you get your work done and if the quality is better.

Disconnecting doesn't hurt

Heart surgeons and emergency response teams may need to be available 24/7 for emergency calls. A high school kid does not. Do you answer texts or email while you're quarterbacking the football team, performing in the school play or giving a speech to run for class president? Of course you don't. Disconnect so you can give the same focus to your studies that you give to these activities.

This skill of eliminating interruptions and letting yourself really focus on your work will be even more valuable in college. If you can be the kind of student who can turn a two-hour break in between classes into effective study time, you'll buy yourself two hours of free time that evening for other projects, activities or good old-fashioned college fun.

When you have important work to do, eliminate all interruptions until you're done. You'll do better work and you'll finish faster. All the emails, texts and Facebook posts will still be there when you're done. And you can reply to all of them without the work hanging over you.

Make academic workouts intense

Two types of members you'll see at the gym are:

1. The one who hits the workout hard for 45 minutes, works out like his hair is on fire, doesn't talk to anyone, and usually leaves tired, sweaty and disgusting.

2. The one who's in no rush to get out of there, who half-heartedly lifts a few weights, talks to people, checks himself out in the mirror, runs a few minutes on a treadmill, watches the TV, repeats the cycle a few times, showers and talks with guys in the locker room about the "brutal two-hour workout" he just finished.

The first member is in much better shape and spends half as much time at the gym as the second guy. He gets more done in less time, with better results because he's focused.

What if you approached your homework and studying like the first gym member?

Rise above the grade grubbers

Counselors, teachers and college admissions officers use a term to describe some students: "Grade grubbers." You don't want to be one.

Grade grubbers are so obsessively focused on their GPAs that they're not interested in learning—they just want the A. They'll only participate in class discussions if participation is counted toward a grade. They'll only do an outside project or extra reading if they get points for it.

When a grade grubber gets a B in the class, he doesn't ask the teacher how he could actually improve his work and do better; he asks what extra credit is available so he can get an A. And if that doesn't work, a grade grubber's parents aren't above waging a "My son needs an A in this class" argument with the teacher and counselor.

It's not that grade grubbers don't work hard. But if all you care about is the grade, and you'll resort to anything to get that grade, it's like volunteering for a community service project just to collect the hours for your resume, not caring at all about the people you're actually helping.

Grade grubbing is a selfish way to go through school. It's hard for teachers and counselors to really like grade grubbers.

FIVE QUESTIONS TO ASK YOUR HIGH SCHOOL COUNSELOR

When you first visit your high school counselor, here are five questions to get your college planning started.

1. Am I taking the right courses to be competitive for college?

2. What are some appropriate colleges for me to look at?

3. Are any college reps visiting our campus this semester?

4. Does the counseling office do any college planning presentations or have any guidance materials that I should take advantage of?

5. Are there any special instructions you like students to follow when requesting transcripts, school reports or anything else from your office?

Love to learn

The opposite of a grade grubber is a kid who loves to learn. Those kids work hard and get good grades, too, but they do so more because of their own curiosity than an agenda to get into prestigious colleges.

It might be a student who loves literature and takes some college-level creative writing courses during the summer; who participates in her English classes and talks to her teacher after school about books; or who's a happy, self-described lit geek who can't wait to join a book club in college so she can stay up late talking Shakespeare with others just like her.

Colleges love students who enjoy learning new things and take initiative to learn them. It doesn't matter whether it's math, literature, science, cooking, automotive repair, computer programming, wood-working, dance—if you find it interesting, feed your curiosity. Show colleges you're not just a high achiever but also a curious learner.

Even if you're not a straight-A student, show colleges what you're capable of when you're learning what you want to learn. A C student who loves his video production class and takes a summer course at a local film school has just given colleges something else to notice besides his GPA.

William's story

One former Collegewise student, William, took this advice. He was a straight-A student who had two passions—science and cooking. When he found a summer course at UC Irvine called "Food Science," it was like someone had created a course just for him. He enrolled (over his mother's urging that he take calculus instead) and later wrote his college essay about how much he loved learning about the chemical reactions that make bread rise and the physics explanation of why adding salt to water makes your spaghetti cook faster.

William was admitted to his first choice—Stanford University.

There's nothing wrong with being focused on your GPA. But real learners see academic rewards as a byproduct of their work ethic and curiosity.

Nobel Prize v. learning

Richard Feynman was a physics professor at Caltech who worked on the atomic bomb and was a member of the team that investigated the Space Shuttle Challenger

If you really were just three points away from an A—and there's no changing your teacher's position—it's a bitter pill to swallow. Also, consider that lots of things, from swim meets to sales competitions at big companies, are based on cold, hard numbers, and you can't win the prize just for getting close. Instead of complaining, find out what you can do differently next time and resolve to do it.

What if the excuse is legitimate?

Sometimes your academic performance suffers for a legitimate reason. At Collegewise we worked with a student whose mother was diagnosed with leukemia during his junior year, and he had to care for her after school. Another student was a baseball player who got hit in the head with a foul ball and had to miss three weeks of school with a serious head injury. Their grades suffered because of real challenges, and they explained those circumstances to colleges when they applied.

It's not complaining when you do face a challenging circumstance that's out of your control. But most excuses for a poor performance in class are just that—excuses. Colleges (and future employers) don't want students who blame other people. They want the students who find solutions and make it work.

How to Thrive in Extracurricular Activities

Choose what you enjoy

Many students have the impression that colleges reward particular activities. The logic suggests a student who hasn't worked at a soup kitchen or served as president of the Latin Club is somehow at a disadvantage in the eyes of the admissions committee. It's not true. College admissions officers don't care which particular activities you choose to do. They're more interested in how much you care about what you're doing.

Colleges appreciate community service and leadership activities, but not more (or less) than success in or passion for athletics, art, music or any other activity that you really care about and make an impact doing. An entire college campus full of nothing but leaders and philanthropists wouldn't be as interesting as a community with lots of different talents and interests.

Jerome Lucido, Provost for Enrollment Policy and Management at the University of Southern California, told The Washington Post, "There simply is no mold for 'what admission directors are looking for.' The important thing is to design your activities to develop and test your interests, not to please a distant admission official. Yes, we believe this!"[21]

If you want to impress colleges, show them that you have the initiative and passion to find things you love doing and then commit yourself to them. Colleges know those students will keep being engaged and involved once they get to college.

Show passion

Some students worry about doing *enough* activities to show colleges. They want to sign up for as many clubs on campus as possible so they can pad their resumes and look involved. But long lists of activities don't impress colleges. Real commitment does.

It's not hard to join a lot of clubs. Anyone can show up to a few meetings just so they can add to the activity sections of their college applications. What's impressive is the student who finds a few activities she really cares about and commits to them. Colleges know it's that committed student, not the compulsive joiner, who's more likely to make the same kinds of contributions once she gets to college.

Tony Bankston, Dean of Admissions at Illinois Wesleyan University told *The Washington Post*, "Students who have a passion for something are significantly more likely to make a more significant contribution to the campus community. They are not only more likely to get involved, but they are also more apt to bring new initiatives to campus or bring about improvements to existing clubs or programs. Passion is more likely to breed action."[23]

Time investment

When you list your activities on your application, most colleges will also ask you to estimate how many days a week, and how many weeks a year, you spend doing each one. That's why the sheer number of activities that you do is less important than the commitment you make to each one.

The tennis player who spends almost all her free time on the court is still impressive to colleges even though she may only be listing one activity on her application. Commitment quality beats activity quantity. Game. Set. Match.

Many colleges, including more than 450 that use the standardized Common Application, also require applicants to write an essay about an activity that's been important to them. The students who have the best answers to that question are always the ones who give a lot of time and energy to do something they care about, whether it's playing water polo, working at an ice cream shop, acting in school plays or taking karate classes.

Hobbies count, too

Hobbies can be activities, too. If you invest a lot of time and energy into a hobby you enjoy, colleges will be impressed (as long as the hobby isn't prohibited by law).

One Collegewise student spent a lot of time fishing. He and his dad would take regular trips together that they'd plan months in advance based on the season and what kind of fish would be likely be biting. During his junior year, he took up spear fishing and spent a lot of time learning how to do it. He wrote his college essay about his hobby and titled it, "Gone Fishin'." Today, he's a graduate of California's Loyola Marymount University.

Choose what you enjoy

I never joined a club at school because none of them appealed to me, and I didn't have the dedication or athleticism for any of the sports. However, I did find a way to be a part of the school community. During my sophomore year, I struggled with anxiety and depression. As a part of my recovery, I volunteered to speak to health classes about my illness. I've spoken to many classes after two years, and it has been among the most rewarding experiences of my life. It helped me get over my anxiety, help people who are struggling with what I went through, and have a subject for a college essay, all in one. I'm glad I found a way to be active and helpful in my school community.

Ben C.
Former Collegewise student, Class of 2012
Western Washington University

So don't worry whether or not you have enough activities. Are you doing things you enjoy? Are you spending quality time and energy to do them? Then relax. What you do within your activities is more important than how many activities you do.

Stand out from the crowd

Have you ever noticed that certain clubs and organizations are particularly crowded? We've met a lot of students who join the Key Club or National Charity League because, well, everyone else seemed to be doing them.

There's nothing wrong with joining any popular activity if that's what you really want to do. But if you're just doing it because everyone else is, why not stop following the crowd and do something different?

We've met a lot of kids who have volunteered at hospitals. But we've only met one who also worked as an emergency medical technician. She wrote her essay about her first night on the job in the back of a speeding ambulance when she did chest compressions on a 19-year-old motorcycle accident victim who had just gone into full cardiac arrest. She got accepted to her first choice—University of San Diego—where she studied psychology.

Lots of kids go to expensive summer programs at colleges. But we've only ever met one who spent his summers taking history classes at his local community colleges for $20 per unit. He got to know one of the professors who shared the reading assignments for her upper division course on George Washington. That student didn't care whether any college would look favorably on it—that's not what it was about for him. He was just obsessed with history and wanted to know more. He went to Yale, where he majored in history, and then to Georgetown Law School.

Lots of kids play an instrument in the high school jazz band. But we've only ever met one who also played trumpet in a real mariachi band. He wasn't doing it to put it on his college applications—he just liked playing good music (and wearing the authentic mariachi outfit). He went to Occidental College and studied economics.

Those students weren't necessarily smarter, more talented or harder working than all their classmates. And they weren't trying to game the process and do things they thought would help them get into college. They just took otherwise common interests to uncommon places.

Bottom line: doing your own thing on your own terms can be a lot more enjoyable than following the crowd—and a better way to stand out.

Need Summer Activity Suggestions?

Colleges will also look at how you spent your summers. If you'd like suggestions, check out The Princeton Review's InBlog at in.princetonreview.com and search for the key word "summer." You'll find a ton of posts offering student perspectives on summer programs, tips on finding a summer job, and even extracurricular reading recommendations. Over on Collegewise's Wise Like Us blog, you can find a post on "50 Ways to Spend Your Summer." It's got a list of potential activities, all of which are free or low cost.

http://www.wiselikeus.com/collegewise/2012/04/
50-ways-to-spend-your-summer.html

Real commitment

You certainly do see what I call "serial participators" who are in every club and organization to either get their picture in the yearbook the most times or perhaps stuff their resume for the college application. That superficial participation can't be sustained in college and is not impressive.[24]

David Lesesne
Dean of Admissions and Financial Aid
Randolph-Macon College

No laundry lists

We are always suspicious of students with laundry lists of extracurricular activities because it suggests that the student is not developing an in-depth engagement with any one activity. Also, it suggests a level of frenetic busyness that may be more about building a college resume than about genuine interests on the part of the student.[25]

Eileen Brangan Mell
Worcester Polytechnic Institute

Make an impact

One of the more popular essay topics colleges now require is some version of, "How will you contribute to our campus community?"

The best responses to that question come from students who aren't just involved in activities, but actually make an impact on the people, teams and organizations they're involved with.

Making an impact means the team, club, job or group is different with you there, and they'd notice if you stopped showing up.

If you're the MVP quarterback, the editor-in-chief of the newspaper or the founder of a successful food drive, you're making an impact. But impact isn't reserved for the superstars. The second stringers, the B students, and the club members without leadership positions can make an impact, too.

The staff writer on the school newspaper could take a journalism class at a college and then offer to share the material with the rest of the writers on the paper once he completes the course.

The second-chair oboe player in the orchestra could convince the conductor of the local community symphony to come to one of their music classes to talk about life as a professional musician.

A B student in physics could organize an all-star team of classmates to compete in the national high school physics Olympics.

Colleges have a term for these kids: "High-impact applicants." They know these students make positive contributions to their classes, organizations and fellow students. People would notice if they stopped showing up.

How a bench warmer made an impact

One former Collegewise student said he was the worst player on his water polo team. He played about three minutes of actual game time in high school. But he ran the fundraiser to buy parkas for the team. He volunteered to hold the video camera when the coach wanted to start recording games. Most importantly, he loved being on the water polo team.

This student brought a great attitude to practice every day even though he knew he'd never play, and he won the coach's award two years in a row. He wasn't a good player, but the team would have missed him if he stopped showing up. He wrote his college essay about his experience as the worst player on the water polo team and was accepted to almost all of his colleges.

If you stopped showing up to your part-time job, soccer practice, rehearsals for the school play or your art class after school, would the group be missing something important?

If not, start looking for opportunities to make an impact. Become indispensible and leave a legacy.

Learn when and how to quit

A lot of students think that once they start an activity, they should never quit because it would look bad to colleges. But colleges don't want you to just plod through something for the sake of sticking it out. Successful people not only know how to commit to things, but also how to quit.

You change a lot while you're in high school. A club or activity you joined as a freshman might lose some of its oomph by the time you're a junior. Good quitters can sense when an activity, a job, a project or a relationship isn't going anyplace good or is just making them unhappy. So they quit and move on, and they don't beat themselves up about it.

One former Collegewise students was a standout football player, but he quit right before the start of his junior year. Football was making him miserable. He realized he just wasn't the type of guy who would ever enjoy, as he put it, "doing something where he was regularly congratulated for trying to take someone's head off."

This student wanted to do other things that he thought would make him happier. So he quit, joined a steel drum band at his high school and started volunteering at his church. He went on to attend and graduate from Notre Dame.

When you give time and effort to an activity, it should give something back to you. If you hate every second of marching band practice and are pretty sure that lugging your tuba around every day after school has caused permanent damage to your spine—stop. Don't march in the band anymore. Find something else that you enjoy with lighter equipment.

COMMITTEE NOTES

Make an impact

Colleges are more interested in the student's passion, the authenticity of the student's involvement, and the impact they've had in their communities, teams, or organizations. Sometimes that means they've only done 1 or 2 things, but they've been involved in a way that has fundamentally impacted those organizations. That to me is more important than being involved in 20 clubs and not having impacted any.[26]

Angel B. Perez
Dean of Admissions
Pitzer College

When quitting pays big

Knowing that quitting is an option can also strengthen your commitment to things you really care about. The online retailer Zappos bribes new employees to quit. "The Offer," as it's known at Zappos, is the brainchild of CEO Tony Hsieh. Every new call center employee at Zappos goes through a four-week training program during which time they earn their full salary. At the end of the program, Zappos offers $4,000 to any new hire who wants to quit. Only about 2–3 percent of the people take the money and run.[27]

By giving new employees an easy way to quit, Zappos fills its ranks with people who really want to be there.

Are you doing an activity that your heart's just not in anymore? If the answer is, "Yes," why are you still doing it? Why not find something you love enough that you'd never take the bribe to quit?

Keep in mind, not all quitting is good. If you love being on the volleyball team, but quit just because you didn't get picked as the starting setter, maybe you should stay and work to earn your spot back?

You get to choose which activities you do outside of class. If you make the wrong choice, or if what used to make you happy just isn't working for you anymore, don't be afraid to be a good quitter and make a different choice.

COMMITTEE NOTES

On good quitting

Sometimes it's refreshing to see the student who, for example, gave up the violin he had been playing for years because he wanted the time to try soccer. Continuity is not a virtue unto itself. Scattered evidence of a curious mind can be more impressive than singular achievements from routinized commitments.[28]

Henry Broaddus
Dean of Admissions
The College of William & Mary

Get a job

One amendment to the rule of thumb that one activity isn't more important than another: every teenager should seriously consider having a part-time job at some point in high school. And not a job you don't have to apply for at your mom or dad's company. A regular, honest-to-goodness, flipping burgers, bagging groceries, ringing a cash register, sweeping the floors kind of job.

Kids who have part-time jobs learn a lot. They learn how to deal with angry customers, how to show initiative and how to work well with people. We've read some wonderful college essays from kids who worked at fast food restaurants and talked about how good it felt when they got promoted to shift manager and didn't have to take orders at the drive-thru anymore.

Every admissions officer we've ever asked about this has agreed it's hard not to like a kid who scoops ice cream or pours coffee or takes tickets at the movie theater to make some extra money.

A teen that gets a regular part-time job almost certainly has no ulterior motive. There's rarely a hidden strategy to impress colleges when a student chooses to serve frozen yogurt part time. You can't always say the same about the kid whose family pays thousands of dollars to send him to summer school at an Ivy League university. All the students we have worked with who discussed their part-time jobs in their applications have been very successful at getting into college.

Job market

There are potential future career advantages to sweeping floors or scooping popcorn at the movies while you're in high school. It's not an easy job market out there for recent college grads. Among the students who graduated from college in 2010, just 56 percent managed to get a job by the following spring. That compares with 90 percent of graduates from the classes of 2006 and 2007.[29] There has been some uptick in employment rates for new grads in the past few years, but given the instability of the global economy, you should look for every opportunity to make yourself desirable to future employers.

Everybody needs their first job at some point—the job you take because you don't have any work experience and know you can't afford to be picky. Why not do that in high school? Get your first job at 16 or 17, and before you even start college, you'll have something to list on your resumé and references you can give potential internships or employers.

CHAPTER 4

Testing:
Planning and Preparing for Standardized Tests

THE HISTORY OF THE SAT AND ACT[2]

1926

Carl Brigham, a psychologist who created aptitude tests for the US Army during World War I, after the war develops the Scholastic Aptitude Test (SAT) for use in college admissions.

1933

Harvard begins using the SAT to evaluate applicants for a new scholarship program.

1939

The SAT introduces new machine-scored answer sheets. While the SAT had always been a multiple-choice test, all of the student responses previously needed to be reviewed and scored by hand.

1958

For the first time, students may see their SAT scores. Before 1958, only high schools and colleges were able to view students' scores.

1959

Everett Franklin Lindquist, an education professor at the University of Iowa, develops the American College Testing Program (ACT) as a competitor to the SAT. In addition to math, reading and English skills, the ACT assesses students on their knowledge of scientific facts and principles.

1971

The College Board begins to mail scores directly to students' homes (they were previously sent to the high schools).

1990

The SAT is renamed so that the acronym stands for "Scholastic Assessment Test."

1993

The SAT is renamed and is no longer an acronym. The letters SAT don't stand for anything.

1996

The ACT (both the test and the company) are renamed. The letters ACT are no longer an acronym—they don't stand for anything.

2001

Richard Atkinson, president of the University of California, tells a group of fellow college presidents, "The SATs have acquired a mystique that's clearly not warranted. Who knows what they measure?" He proposes the university make SAT scores an optional part of the application for all 90,000 kids who apply each year.

2005

Partly in response to the University of California criticisms, the content of the SAT is changed. Verbal analogy questions are dropped and a writing skills section with an essay is added.

Students now get three SAT scores—Critical Reading, Math and Writing—each on a scale of 200–800. A perfect score is now 2400.

2007

Harvey Mudd College begins accepting ACT scores. The ACT is now a valid admissions test at every four-year college and university in the United States.

2009

Score Choice is introduced for the SAT, allowing students to decide which scores from multiple administrations will be sent to colleges.

2010

The number of high school seniors taking the ACT (1.57 million) is greater than those taking the SAT (1.55 million).

Learn your testing ABCs

Before we get into which tests to take, when to take them and how to maintain your testing perspective, let's define some terms. Below are five standardized tests you'll need to make decisions about taking. More on how to decide in "Pick a test and go with it."

1. PSAT

The PSAT is a practice version of the SAT. It covers the same three skills categories, but is shorter than the SAT. It's given in October at your high school and is intended to be an optional, nonthreatening opportunity to see how you might score on the SAT without having to sit for the real thing. The PSAT is also used as a qualifier for National Merit scholarships, which is good news for good test takers, but it's never used for college admissions purposes. It consists of five sections, which are always given in the same order:

Section	Number of Questions	Time
Critical Reading	24	25 minutes
Math	20	25 minutes
Critical Reading	24	25 minutes
Math	18	25 minutes
Writing Skills	39	30 minutes

You'll receive three scores for the PSAT, one each for Critical Reading, Math, and Writing Skills. Each of these scores is reported on a scale of 20 to 80. Your scores will be mailed to your high school principal, who will distribute them six to eight weeks after you take the test (if you're homeschooled, your score report will be sent directly to you). The College Board has announced some changes to the test for 2015, which you can learn more about on our website or at www.collegeboard.com.

2. PLAN/Aspire

The PLAN is a practice test for the ACT. It's less popular than the PSAT, and high schools that offer it traditionally do so for sophomores. Like the PSAT, it's just a practice test and doesn't impact your chances of getting into college. In spring of 2014, ACT, Inc. is rolling out a new system called Aspire, a computer-based system to assess a student's progress through elementary and early high school. You can learn more about Aspire and the transition away from the PLAN at www.discoveractaspire.org.

3. SAT

The SAT will be undergoing big changes in 2016, so it's important that you visit www.collegeboard.com and www.PrincetonReview.com/sat for the most up-to-date information. The the current exam has ten sections covering three areas of skill–Math, Critical Reading, and Writing (which also includes an essay). The sections include:

- One 25-minute Essay section, requiring you to present your viewpoint on a given topic

- Two 25-minute Math sections, one containing multiple choice questions and the other containing multiple choice questions and response questions for which you will "grid-in" your answer

- Two 25-minute Critical Reading sections, made up of sentence completions and reading comprehension questions

- One 25-minute Writing section, containing error identification questions, improving sentences questions, and improving paragraphs questions

- One 20-minute Math section, including only multiple choice questions

- One 20-minute Critical Reading section, again featuring sentence completions and reading comprehension questions

- One 10-minute Writing section, containing only improving sentences questions

- One 25-minute Experimental section, which may be Writing, Math, or Critical Reading. There's no way to tell which section is the Experimental section, so you should approach every section as if it will be scored.

Each skill area receives a score between 200–800. The lowest possible overall score you can get is 600, the highest is 2400. The national average score is about 1500 (500 in each section).

4. ACT

Meet the Pepsi to SAT's Coke—the ACT. The ACT and SAT are two companies with competing products that are used for exactly the same purposes, and similarly, the ACT is changing and going digital in 2015. Visit www.act.org and www. PrincetonReview.com/act for up-to-date information. The current ACT has four sections: English, Reading, Math and Science. There's also an optional 30-minute essay (which you should do unless you're 100 percent certain that your chosen colleges don't want it). Each of the four sections is scored from 1–36, then they average the four scores together for your "composite score" between 1 and 36. The composite score is what you'll quote when a nosey friend asks, "What'd you get on the ACT?" The national average is about 21.

Colleges that require standardized tests will accept either the SAT or the ACT. And they never require you to take both.

5. Subject Tests

SAT subject tests are one-hour tests that focus on specific academic subjects. There are 20 tests in five different areas—Math, History, Literature, Science and Languages. Each subject test is scored from 200–800. You can find a listing of all the tests at www.collegeboard.com.

About 30 colleges—most of them highly competitive—require some combination of subject tests (e.g., Math Level 1 or Level 2, and a science). Roughly 25 colleges recommend—but don't require—subject tests. And some 50 schools neither require nor recommend subject tests but are happy to look at your scores if you choose to send them.

If you're taking a challenging curriculum, especially one that includes honors or AP classes, consider taking the corresponding subject tests in your strongest subjects.

Don't panic over PSAT scores

Testing panic tends to start building in December or January of high school students' junior year, when they get their PSAT scores back. It's scary to get your first big-name standardized test score, and it's easy to let anything less than a great score freak you out. I've been invited to speak at "PSAT scores-back nights" at high schools where students receive their scores surrounded by counselors, parents and several hundred of their closest friends. (No pressure.)

Relax and remember that the PSAT is just a practice test. It's like a dress rehearsal before opening night of the play. That's all. It was created to let students take a nonthreatening trial version of the SAT before they take the real thing. It can't hurt you. It can't damage your future. No student in the history of college admissions has ever been rejected by a college because she scored poorly on the PSAT.

Yes, a small number of students (about 8,000 of the 1.5 million annual test takers[3]) are awarded National Merit scholarships every year, and the PSAT scores are the first of many rounds of qualifiers. If you're notified that your PSAT scores qualify you for future consideration, that's good news. (Unless you don't like free cash.)

How colleges use PSAT scores

The only thing colleges use PSAT scores for is marketing—they buy the names of those who sit for it, so they can mail them marketing materials. If you recently took the test and checked the box that you would like to receive information from colleges, you and your mail carrier will soon see what I mean.

According to the College Board's website, more than 1,100 colleges, universities and scholarship programs[4] pay them (at a base price of $0.37 per name[5]) for student contact information, and the PSAT is one source from which they harvest the list.

How to use your PSAT scores

If you did well on the PSAT, it's good news because you will likely do well on the SAT when you take it. But for everyone else, use your PSAT scores constructively.

Maybe low PSAT scores are your first sign that you might be a better ACT taker? Or maybe you can use your PSAT score to identify the parts of the test that have you the most troubled so you can focus on those areas when you prepare for the SAT. Or use the score sheet to practice your origami swan. Those are good ways to use your PSAT scores.

Keep tests in perspective

Nowhere in the world of college admissions has more of the population gone so far over the deep end as they have with standardized test anxiety and the resulting preparation. Seventh graders are taking SAT prep classes. Families take tutors with them on vacation so as not to break a test preparation streak. Be careful. You're bound to meet these people and they will either make you feel bad about your testing approach, or scare the hell out of you. You don't need to drive yourself crazy: These tests are coachable, crackable, and conquerable, and the Princeton Review has helped millions of students raise their scores on all kinds of standardized tests for more than 20 years. We offer a huge range of test prep products to suit the needs of just about any student.

confirmed that for the vast majority of the university's graduates who scored in the middle range of the test as high school students, the ACT explained only 3.6 percent of the differences in cumulative college GPA.[12]

Standardized tests measure how well you take standardized tests. That's about it. There are good test takers and bad test takers, and they sometimes have wildly overlapping levels of academic achievement. This is a good thing: It means that with some preparation, you can score well on these tests, regardless of the grades you might have received in related subject areas.

The natural question is, of course: *why do so many colleges require standardized tests?*

They require them because they want a common yardstick to compare students with 3.5 GPAs from Toledo, Tallahassee, Tacoma, and every other city in the United States, not to mention international applicants.

Those kids earned their 3.5 GPAs from different high schools (and home schools) with different requirements and different teachers. But they all take the same standardized tests. It's a far-from-perfect system to compare kids; but for now, the tests remain a necessary evil. Or rather, a rite of passage.

Kid to Kid

Test scores don't measure how smart you are

I was a 4.0 student, but I have always been a bad test taker and I knew that I would struggle with the ACT and SAT. I did many practice tests and had a tutor for the ACT, but the three times I took it, I got an average score every time. This was extremely frustrating, but it wasn't the end of the world. My advice is that students need to put their best effort into getting good grades. Having a higher GPA and lower test scores is better than having a lower GPA and higher test scores.

Kyla S.
Former Collegewise student, Class of 2012
Chapman University

If you're a good test taker, congratulations. You have one less thing to worry about and you should show off that skill by nailing your standardized tests.

If you're not a good test taker, I encourage you (and your parents) to not take your scores personally. Don't let subpar scores make you feel badly about yourself. And please don't obsess so much about transforming yourself into a good test taker that you ignore school, the jazz band, your community service work or anything else more important to you and to many colleges. But do take advantage of the test prep tools available. The Princeton Review offers books, tutoring, and classes both in person and online. And the College Board website offers a free practice test so you can check out how you might score.

Plan your testing calendar

A quick way to get stressed about college admissions is to get to your senior year and realize you've neglected to take a standardized test that one of your chosen colleges requires.

Here's a suggested timeline to avoid that.

Now

1. Visit the websites of any colleges you are considering and review their testing requirements. This is a good way to get an admissions context for the testing plans you're about to make.

Sophomore Year

1. Take the PSAT or the PLAN—whichever one your school offers—in October. These are both nonthreatening practice tests that will make it easier for you to decide between the SAT and the ACT when the time comes to choose.

2. If you are a strong student with goals to attend a selective college, consider taking Subject Tests in June for the related courses you're completing. For example, if you're taking biology and doing well in it, you'll never know that material better than you will as you're preparing for final exams. That's the perfect time to take the Biology Subject Test.

Even if your research in Step No. 1 indicated that none of your colleges require Subject Tests, you might still consider taking them at the appropriate times in case you later add schools to your list that do want them.

Junior Year

1. Take the PSAT in October of your junior year. It will help you decide between the SAT or ACT, and how much you should prepare for either, this spring.

2. Prepare for and take either the SAT or ACT (but not both) at least once during your junior year.

3. Consider taking Subject Tests in May or June for the related courses you're completing.

Senior Year

1. In the fall of your senior year, retake the SAT or ACT if you need to improve your scores.

Before you actually enact this plan, review it with your high school counselor. I recommend this for two reasons. First, it's good to involve your counselor in your college planning, and to show her that you're the type of student who gets organized and seeks out advice. Second, your counselor may suggest that you alter this calendar slightly. For example, I've worked with students whose schools offered "life science" instead of "biology," which impacted their chances of scoring well on a biology subject test.

What if you're starting late?

If you're reading this in the fall of your senior year and you've yet to take any tests, all is not lost. Research the testing requirements of your schools to find out what you need to take, and find out the date by which those scores need to be submitted to your chosen colleges. The SAT, Subject Tests and ACT are given in October, November and December, and most schools will accept scores from those dates.

Pick a test and go with it

Every college in the country that requires standardized tests scores will accept either the SAT or the ACT. That hasn't always been the case (e.g., Harvey Mudd College held out on accepting the ACT until January 2007), but today, you will not find a four-year college in the United States that requires both the SAT and the ACT, and you will not find school that accepts one test but not the other.

So you have a choice—SAT or ACT—and an opportunity to play to your testing strengths by focusing only on the test you're naturally better at. That's the good news. Unfortunately, when you compare the features and benefits of the SAT and ACT, it's nearly impossible to decode which one is better for you. See for yourself:

SAT vs. ACT comparison

	SAT	ACT
Sections	Math, Writing, Critical Reading	Math, English, Reading, Science
Scoring	Sections scored from 200-800 and then added together. The highest score is 2400.	Sections scored from 1 to 36, then averaged for a composite score out of 36.
Essay	Yes	Optional
Math	Arithmetic, Algebra, and Geometry	Arithmetic, Algebra, Geometry, and Trigonometry
Tests vocabulary?	Yes	No
Points deducted for wrong answers?	Yes	No

How to choose

If you've taken both the PLAN and the PSAT, you can compare your scores of those two exams and see if you're better at one over the other.

If you haven't taken one or both of those tests, you can contact your local Princeton Review office and take a free PRA (Princeton Review Assessment), which will help you determine if you will score higher on the SAT or ACT. Here are seven key differences between the exams:

TEST TIPS FOR THE SELF-GUIDED PREPPER

- Make a pledge to do one or two sections of SAT problems every day. That's just 25 to 50 minutes, so make the time. Do practice questions instead of watching bad TV shows.

- Practice under timed conditions if the SAT is less than 2 weeks away—you want to get used to working against the clock.

- Don't be afraid to go back and review any of the lessons that you think you need more work on. The techniques work, but only if you understand when and how to use them.

- Get into a regular sleep cycle. Go to bed around the same time every night, and get up earlier on weekends. You want to train your body to be awake on Saturdays.

- Take a full-length SAT on a Saturday morning. You need the stamina to sit through a three-hour, forty-five-minute test.

- Take an index card and write math formulas on one side and verbal strategies on the other side. Study them whenever you have a spare moment.

So, how do you know when to throw in the testing towel and put the SAT or ACT behind you? There's only a little hard science to this decision, but here are a few guidelines.

1. Did you nail it?

If you met or beat what you hoped you could score, move on. End your standardized testing career on a high note. We know it's tempting to think you might be able to eke out even more points, but there are lots of other things you can be doing to prepare for college admissions that are more important, and more rewarding, than doing more test prep.

Also, if you scored 2150 or higher on the SAT, or 32 or higher on the ACT, walk away. Those scores are good enough at even the most selective schools. Higher scores won't improve your chances, and taking the test again just makes you look neurotic.

2. Check average test scores.

Most colleges share the average test scores of the students they admit. You can find that information on their websites or on collegeboard.com. Before you make a decision about retesting, it's good to know how you compare to students your chosen colleges admit.

Also, don't forget that many colleges allow you to report your highest SAT Math, Critical Reading and Writing scores from different sittings (a practice called "superscoring"). So your highest test score may be better than you thought it was.

Here's an example. Let's say you take the SAT twice and get the following scores:

630 Math	590 Math
520 Critical Reading	660 Critical Reading
600 Writing	640 Writing
Total score: 1750	**Total score: 1890**

Your best SAT score from one sitting is 1890. But if the schools you're applying to look at your highest scores for each section from different sittings, your score is actually 1930 (630 Math from the first sitting, 660 Critical Reading and 640 Writing from the second sitting).

Some schools use a similar practice for ACT scores, but not nearly as many as do for the SAT. Visit the admissions sections on the websites of the colleges that interest you and find out how they use the scores. Then you can make an informed decision about taking the test again.

3. What does your counselor say?

Once you have the information about your colleges' average test scores of admitted students, visit your high school counselor and ask for her opinion about whether to take the test again. Test scores are more important at some colleges than they are at others. Your counselor can also take other factors into account, like how strong your curriculum and grades are, to give you good advice about whether or not you really need higher test scores.

4. Are you feeling optimistic, or beaten down?

Some students want to take the test again because they know they can do better. They feel they've got the testing upper hand and want to show what they can do. If you're feeling buoyed and want one more try at slaying the testing beast, have at it. But if you've done your best and spent your time preparing and now just wish you never have to take them again, do something else that doesn't make you feel so discouraged.

For most students who plan and prepare well, two times is enough for any standardized tests. When a student decides he's just got to try a third time, I tell him to go for it, but then mandate that he throw in the testing towel once he finishes. Part of managing standardized tests means knowing when to say when.

Realize your test scores soon won't matter

Test scores deserve some reasonable concern during your high school years, but not nail-biting stress. Here's the futility of it all: one day in the not-too-distant future, nobody will care what your SAT and ACT scores were.

Once you leave high school, SAT and ACT scores are ancient history. Nobody will care how you did. If you struggled with these tests, you'll laugh about them, not unlike the way some people have to laugh about the terrible fashion or hairstyles they chose during their teen years. Good or bad, it's ancient high school history. You move on after graduation.

Nobody has ever become a failure in life because his or her test scores weren't high enough. Millions of students with all levels of test scores have gone to college. What happens after that will have nothing to do with how you scored on those tests. Your college friends won't know or care. You will never interview for a job where someone asks you what your SAT scores were. The person you eventually want to marry isn't going to dump you if you reveal that you got low test scores back in high school.

SAT and ACT scores have an influence in your life right now. But the expiration date for their influence is coming soon. 🎓

POST-TRAUMATIC TEST DISORDER

Let test scores be ancient history

It has taken 20 years to forget the trauma of that damned test (the SAT), and looking up my scores would be like going back to Vietnam.[13]

Conan O'Brien
Late night television host
Harvard graduate

TEST TIPS FOR THE NIGHT BEFORE AND THE DAY OF THE TEST

The Friday before the big day, just relax. Trying to cram tonight will just make you nervous. You've spent plenty of time getting ready for the SAT, so one more night isn't going to make a big difference. Find something else to think about. Hang out with friends or go see an early movie.

This is not the night to begin experimenting with something new. Go to bed at a reasonable hour, but don't try going to sleep at 7:00. You'll just lie there and think about the test. You should be ready for the SAT by now, so try not to think too much about it.

On Saturday morning, eat something, but don't go crazy. Steak & eggs won't sit well if you're used to a cup of yogurt. Avoid caffeine. It's a diuretic.

Dress in layers and wear comfortable clothing.

Leave extra time to get to the test center—nobody ever got stressed out by arriving early.

Plan to arrive at the test center between 7:45 a.m. and 8:00 a.m., and find out where you're supposed to go. Use the bathroom if you need to. You will get a short break at the end of each hour of testing time, but you may not be able to leave the room during every break.

Take a few seconds at the beginning of each section to think about your strategy. These thoughts should be running through your head:

How many questions am I going to do? How am I going to approach them?

Also, insist on a comfortable testing environment. If you're left-handed you should have a left-handed desk, or a desk with a large writing surface. Too hot? Too cold? Too noisy? The proctor didn't give you your breaks, or accidentally cut five minutes off of section 5? The kid next to you is making noise?

Speak up, firmly but politely. Tell the proctor while they can still do something about it. They may not be able to solve every problem, but don't be afraid to ask.

Once you've finished the test, *let it go*. Don't spend the next 6 weeks obsessing. Remember, different SATs are scored slightly differently. If it's a really hard test, the scoring curve will be more generous.

5.

Applying:
The Art of
College Applications

 Students are usually in shock when I chuckle and tell them I never expect perfection. In fact, I prefer they not project it in their college applications. Of course, this goes against everything they've been told and makes young people uncomfortable. How could a dean of admissions at one of America's most selective institutions not want the best and the brightest? The reality is, perfection doesn't exist, and we don't expect to see it in a college application. In fact, admissions officers tend to be skeptical of students who present themselves as individuals without flaws.[1] **"**

Angel B. Perez
Dean of Admissions
Pitzer College

Applying:

The Art of College Applications

Part I: It gets personal

Look inside the admissions office

Many large state universities ask for nothing more than a simple application with your biographical and contact information, and copies of both your transcript and test scores. At those schools, the evaluation is a number-crunching exercise. If you've taken the required classes, gotten the minimum GPA and test scores, you're in. The only application strategies for those schools are to fill out the information accurately and to submit everything before the deadlines.

Most of the advice in this chapter is aimed at the more selective colleges—including many competitive public schools—that ask for more personal information in their applications. Most ask you to list your activities and to note how much time you spend doing each of them. Many ask you to write one or more essays. Some invite you to submit letters of recommendation from teachers and counselors and to interview.

Classes, grades, and test scores are always important, but these more comprehensive applications mean more personal evaluations. The admissions officers don't just crunch your numbers—they use your application to get sense of who you are and how you might contribute on campus. How you present yourself can make a big difference.

The application review process

Most selective colleges (schools who admit less than 75 percent of their applicants) use some version of the following process to evaluate applicants.

In the fall as the applications begin to arrive, colleges have full-time administrative staff members who first receive and sort the various pieces and parts (applications, test scores, transcripts and letters of recommendation—all of which are sent at different times by different people) into each applicant's file. This can be a Herculean task. At Vanderbilt University, each complete file consists of about

15 pieces of paper. In 2012, the school reported that it received more than 28,000 applications, amounting to more than 420,000 pieces of paper that needed to be downloaded, printed, sorted and filed.

Once a file is complete, it's handed off to an admissions officer (a "reader"). It's common for colleges to group applications by geographic region so that each reader is evaluating students from a particular territory, allowing readers to get familiar with the high schools in their assigned areas.

First read

Most readers start by reviewing the rigor of your classes, the grades you've earned, your academic standing in your class, and your test scores. They'll look through your list of activities and try to get a sense of which ones meant the most to you. They'll read through your essays to get to know you a little better, read your letters of recommendation and consult your interviewer's report. During this time, readers take notes on each part of the application, and they conclude by writing a summary of your strengths and weaknesses, and anything else that was interesting or notable about you. This process can take anywhere from 20 minutes to an hour, depending on the school and how many pieces of information are part of the application.

At most schools, this first reader can recommend to admit a particularly strong student or to deny one who has no chance of admission, without discussing the applicant with the rest of the committee.

If you're the high school valedictorian and you're applying to a school that accepts B students, you have a good chance at admission unless there is a compelling reason not to, like a suspension from school or a shoddy application that makes it clear you're not interested.

If you apply to MIT and you have multiple D's on your transcript, you're not likely to make it past this first reading.

At most schools, a senior admissions officer has to approve this quick admit or deny it before the decision is made, but there's generally no further discussion with the committee.

The second read

If you make it past the first read, a second reader will review your application, write comments, and compare her impressions of you with those of the first reader. If both readers have the same recommendation (admit or deny), a senior admissions officer will review the file and decide whether to accept the recommendation or to send it to the committee. All other applicants will be sent to the committee for discussion.

The earlier you apply, the sooner you get your answer (and the fewer spaces are left to fill). Rolling admissions isn't an option you choose; it's just something that certain colleges do.

3. Early acceptance options

There are two different early acceptance options that allow you to submit an application by November 1 or 15 of the senior year and receive a decision by December 15.

- **Early Decision**
  Early decision applicants make a binding promise to the college—if you're accepted, you must enroll. In fact, students accepted to a binding early decision program actually have to withdraw all their applications from all other colleges. You can apply to as many other schools as you'd like, but because of this binding commitment, you can only have one early decision school.

  What would happen if a student backed out of an early decision admission? The truth is a college can't legally make you attend. But unless you can demonstrate financial hardship (which is the one reason they will let you back out), colleges have been known to carry a grudge. It's not unusual for an admissions officer to call her colleagues at an applicant's other colleges to let them know he backed out of an early decision commitment.

  Don't mess around with early decision commitments. As part of an early decision application, you, your parents and your counselor all sign a document saying that you understand what you're agreeing to. Backing out will always have consequences.

- **Early Action**
  Early action is just like early decision, but without the binding commitment. Since there's no promise to attend if you're admitted, you can apply to as many early action schools as you'd like, though some schools (most notably Harvard, Yale, Princeton and Stanford) offer "Single Choice Early Action" which, while not binding, limits you from applying to any other early programs, binding or nonbinding.

If you need to take an aspirin, I understand. It starts to sound like a complex logic game.

APPLICATION OPTIONS

Application type	*Deadline	Is the decision binding?	If you're accepted, when do you decide?	Sample schools
Regular admissions	On or around January 1	No	May 1	Most schools offer this option
Rolling admissions	Colleges begin taking applications as early as August 15 and continue as late as March 1	No	May 1	Indiana University, Penn State
Early decision	November 1 or November 15	Yes	N/A. If you're accepted, you're going.	Colgate, Duke
Early action	November 1 or November 15	No	May 1	University of Chicago, Villanova

*These are approximates—you should always check the deadlines for your specific schools.

Seek early decision if...

Many students and parents are told that applying to a binding early decision program can improve their chances of getting in. They don't want to miss out on that advantage, so they feel pressured to apply early. Truth is: the extra stress may not be worth it, unless you know beyond the shadow of a doubt that this is your first choice school.

Applying to a nonbinding early action program does not improve your chances at most colleges. In recent years, colleges that offered an early action option admitted those students at a nearly identical rate as those admitted in the regular pool.[4]

Applying early decision, however, can give you a nice admissions boost at some schools. Nationally, early decision schools admitted 57 percent of early applicants compared with 50 percent in the regular pool in 2010.[5] At some schools, the difference is more dramatic. According to the data Duke reported for 2012, the school accepted 26 percent of early decision applicants and 16 percent of applicants in the regular decision pool.

That's compelling data, but it's important to understand why those admissions rates are higher before you let a potential admissions advantage convince you to apply early decision.

Early applicants are admitted at higher rates because it removes some of the guesswork for colleges. Whoever they admit early is bound to attend—the college won't lose any of those students to other schools. The most selective schools receive two to three times the number of qualified applicants than they could enroll. Most of those applicants also apply to other highly selective colleges. Admitting a higher percentage of students in the early decision pool has more to do with the college snatching up who they want the most than it does with admitting people who aren't qualified.

Advantage: strongest applicants

In our experience, the students who enjoy an early admission advantage are those who are already highly qualified and would probably be admitted in the regular pool, too.

Just because something gets easier doesn't mean it's easier for everybody. Coors Field in Denver has a reputation as the most hitter-friendly park in Major League Baseball. That's great news for Alex Rodriguez (who's hit more than 600 home runs in his career), but it wouldn't help someone who's happy to get a solid base hit in the annual softball friendly.

A student who is a great match for an early decision college, who would be competitive even in the regular pool, and most importantly, who is absolutely certain that she's found her collegiate soulmate, might enjoy an admissions advantage applying early decision. If you fit those three criteria, talk it over with your high school counselor and strongly consider the option.

Otherwise, don't feel pressured to apply early just for the potential admissions boost.

Apply strategically

Once you've identified which application plans are offered by your chosen colleges, here's how to choose the right plan and decide which applications to do first.

1. **Submit rolling applications first.**

Many students can begin their senior year having already received an acceptance from a rolling admissions school. Talk about a nice emotional boost. Imagine knowing for sure you have at least one college to attend before you've even finished the bulk of your applications. That's why it's a good idea for students to complete their rolling applications first, even if those schools are far from their first choices. Your chances of admission will be stronger because there are a lot more spots available at the beginning of the admissions cycle than there are at the end of it (and you never know when the class will fill up).

2. **Apply early (binding or nonbinding) only if you're a competitive applicant.**

When you apply early, you're evaluated based on what you've accomplished by early November. What if you get your best GPA in the first semester of your senior year? What if you retake the SAT in December and improve your score by 120 points? What if you win a debate tournament or get named MVP of the field hockey team or receive a department award in physics?

Early admissions decisions will likely be made before a college can consider any of those accomplishments. If you're not confident, why not do everything you can to have your best semester yet? Nothing improves your chances more than improving your qualifications.

3. **If you apply early, keep working on your other applications.**

College applications are a lot of work (obviously), and it can be tempting for students who submit early applications in November to wait with their fingers crossed, leaving all their other college applications to wait until they heard back from their early school.

Sure, that's a great system if you get an early acceptance. But if you don't, you'll have to muster the enthusiasm to put all the necessary love and attention into finishing your remaining college applications, get them done in just a few weeks over your holiday break, all while nursing the emotional hangover from having a dream school reject you.

Don't do that to yourself. Complete all of your college applications before your holiday break. If your early school says "No," you'll be able to take some solace in the fact that at least your other applications have already been submitted.

Yes, if your dream school admits you, you'll have completely wasted your time on those other applications. But which problem would you rather have?

Help readers know you

The function of your college essay is not to convince the college that you're worthy of admission. It's to help readers get to know you.

Think of your college application and the accompanying essays as doing two separate but equally important jobs. The application—the transcript, standardized test scores, extracurricular activities, honors and awards and letters of recommendation—helps a college decide whether or not you're qualified for admittance. The essays help them decide whether or not they like you.

Colleges know they aren't just admitting collections of grades, test scores and activities. They're admitting real human beings who will live and learn with a community of fellow students. They want to know how you'll fit in.

A high school valedictorian with perfect test scores and a certificate proclaiming that he founded his own country is obviously qualified. But if he seems like an arrogant jerk, a college owes it to the other students to admit a different valedictorian who seems more pleasant to be around.

Colleges ask you to write essays as a way to get to know you in ways that qualifications alone can't do. One of our students wrote about how much he loved his beat up, rusty 1988 Nissan Sentra even though it only started 60 percent of the time and had a heater that would not shut off. That essay helped him relay that he was relaxed, self-assured and likeable. He let the application do the convincing and the essay do the engaging.

One of our counselors who worked in admissions at several selective colleges described it this way: "When reading the essays, I would be asking myself, 'If I were back in college, would I want this kid to be my roommate?'"

COMMITTEE NOTES

Almost the worst thing is for students to write to what they think we are looking for. The best thing they can do is write from the heart.[7]

Stu Schmill
Interim Admissions Director
MIT

The best way to get people to like you is to just be yourself. It's one of those clichés that's true. So don't use the essays to try to convince the college to admit you. Just answer the questions honestly and be yourself. The application tells the college about your qualifications. The essays tell them about the person behind those qualifications.

Kid to Kid

Just be yourself

Many students stress about their college essays and I did, too. But now that I think about it, college essays are fun because you are writing about yourself and showing what you're passionate about. Just be yourself. Write like how you would talk to someone. When you write about who you are, the colleges that accept you are the right places for you because they really like you.

Kyla S.
Former Collegewise student, Class of 2012
Chapman University

Keep the focus on you

Every college essay prompt is designed to yield more about the same subject—you. If your essays don't help readers learn about you, you're focusing on the wrong things.

If you write an essay about how wonderful your English teacher is, you're drifting away from the most important subject. The college will learn a lot more about your English teacher than they will about you.

If you write an essay about how great the other students were at the leadership camp you attended, or how your best friend has always been there for you, or what your dad does for a living, the college is learning about people other than you. They might be impressed by the person you discuss. But that's not the desired outcome here.

Most seventeen-year-olds don't have a story that absolutely no other applicant could share. But your experience playing on the basketball team, running for student body treasurer, going on a family vacation in an RV, volunteering at a hospital, or working a part-time job are not the same as every other kid who had those experiences. Details help you take ownership of a story and make it yours.

For example, a cross-country runner doesn't own: "Cross country is a grueling sport. During the summer, I ran seven miles a day just to get ready for the season."

But she would own: "Last summer, I ran the seven-mile loop through the hills behind my house so many times that the park ranger actually knew my name. (I know hers now, too—it's Karla.) When I was gone for five days on vacation with my family, Karla later told me she'd started worrying that something might have happened to me on the trail. She actually considered doing a search."

If you can't come up with enough details to own a story, it's probably not the right choice for a college essay. That doesn't mean the subject wasn't valuable in some way. If you played varsity basketball for two years and loved every minute of it, list it proudly on your application. But if you can't think of a basketball-related story you own, pick a different topic for your essay.

Keep it fresh

A lot of students write essays about something mentioned elsewhere in their application just to make sure the admissions office notices it. Unless that essay shares something new, it's like repeating a joke to see if you can get a bigger laugh from your audience.

College essays should share new information the admissions office wouldn't know from just reading your application. Colleges know that editors of school newspapers have to work well with people. They know helping the less fortunate feels good, football is hard, and England is different from the United States. Sharing stories the colleges already know just wastes an opportunity to help them get to know you better.

The best ways to make sure your essays don't repeat information:
- Pick a topic that has not been mentioned anywhere on your application, or
- Share new information about something you already listed.

FIVE OF OUR ALL-TIME FAVORITE ESSAYS

1. Jack P. opened his essay with a description of the snow cone business he started at age 10 with his little brothers, a business whose original sign—complete with the unfortunate typo, "Snow Cons"—was still stored in their garage. It was a charming start to an otherwise serious essay, and the detail ensured that no other essay in the stack of applications would start exactly the same way. He went to Princeton.

2. Chad M. wrote an essay about his favorite player on the soccer team he coached for mentally challenged kids, Steven. He admitted that coaches weren't supposed to have favorites, but Chad just couldn't help himself. Steven was his brother. The admissions committee never would have known about Chad's special relationship with his brother had he not shared it in his essay. Chad went to the Air Force Academy.

3. Mike M. wrote about working part time at a hamburger stand throughout high school. That essay began, "I make a mean hamburger. In fact, I'm a professional. I've got four years of professional hamburger-making experience." He'd been the lead in several school plays and was applying as a drama major, but his essay let the reader learn about another activity that had become just as important to him, even if it wasn't as impressive as his acting credentials. He attended USC (University of Southern California).

4. Sarah S. wrote that while she had never been on a date, she was still a proud, fully fledged nerd, one who couldn't wait to attend a college where every lunch table was full of "eligible nerd bachelors." She titled her essay, "I'm with The Banned." We can't imagine anybody reading that essay and not liking a kid so self-aware and comfortable in her own skin. Sarah went to Occidental College.

5. Harry K.'s essay began, "I can balance a shot glass on my head." But he had never had a drink. The shot glass balancing act was part of traditional Greek dancing, an art form he taught to little kids at his Greek church. We can only imagine what a welcome relief it must have been for admissions officers to read an essay about an activity they hadn't already read about from countless other applicants. Harry went on to Yale and then to Georgetown Law School.

One Collegewise student, Raquel, wrote an essay sharing that her festive family loved celebrating together so much, they were the only Mexican family she'd ever known who threw an annual St. Patrick's Day party, one to which her grandmother always arrived with her Chihuahua, "Chiquita," in tow.

Colleges didn't need Raquel to explain the concept that family is important. But the great lengths to which her extended family would go just to spend time together was brand new information colleges never would have known.

Another Collegewise student, Kenny, was a proud Boy Scout. He wrote an essay about the fact that his friends had nicknamed him "Dr. Kenny" because he carried a first-aid kit with him everywhere he went.

The colleges already knew Kenny was a Boy Scout because he'd listed it on the application. They didn't need him to explain what Boy Scouts do. But the story about Kenny carrying the first-aid kid everywhere he went (and the surprising number of times it had come in handy), was new information.

Repeating a story in an essay is like serving leftovers at a dinner party. Keep it fresh and give your reader something new to chew on.

Avoid clichés

One of our counselors referred to his last year working in admissions at Caltech as the year of the blood drive essay. That year, an unusually high number of applicants told the same tale of how one on-campus blood drive changed their lives and made them appreciate the importance of serving humanity.

Writing such grandiose statements into your essays won't help you stand out. The statements sound cliché. So here are the five most overused clichés we—and every admissions officer we've spoken with—see most often, and which you should avoid.

1. The aforementioned "blood drive essay," or "How community service taught me the importance of helping others"

Colleges appreciate students who are concerned about their communities. But one blood drive does not a humanitarian make. A claim to have learned how important it is to help people needs to be substantiated with evidence of a sincere, long-term commitment to helping people. Otherwise, your message loses some oomph.

BAD ESSAY ADVICE

1. **"Use a hook to grab their attention."**

   A "hook" is usually a writer's attempt to inject drama, shock or suspense into the opening of their essay. All too often, it just comes off as trying too hard. "As I crouched into my starter's block, eyes fixed on the icy pool below me, I could feel the tense eyes of the crowd bearing down upon me in my Speedo..."

   What swimmer actually thinks like that before a race? Good stories that are well written don't need hooks. Just say it. You're not fishing here.

2. **"Start your essay with a famous quote."**

   Terrible advice. Admissions officers want to hear from you, not Socrates, Mother Teresa or John F. Kennedy. The exception to the quote rule is if you're quoting a person from your own life who is central to the story (and probably not famous), like, "My baseball coach always says, 'We're going to play smart baseball, gentlemen, because dumb baseball is no fun to play and even worse to watch.'"

   That's personal and it makes the story more interesting.

3. **"Avoid controversial topics."**

   What's controversial to one person may not be controversial to another. If a student spent two semesters volunteering for an organization committed to protecting women's reproductive rights, that story shouldn't be discarded just because some people might not agree with her politics.

   Don't write anything just for the sake of shocking your reader. Don't shy away from a topic that's important to you, either. If you're not sure whether a topic is appropriate, ask your high school counselor for a second opinion.

4. **"Use your essay to highlight your interest in the school."**

   Showing interest in a school is good. But what if the prompt is, "Describe a time you failed or made a mistake"? How are you going to tie that to your interest in Gettysburg College?

If a college wants to know about your interest, they'll ask. If a topic you choose actually does have something to do with the reason you're applying, feel free to discuss it. But don't wedge it into your essay unnecessarily.

5. **"Use your essay to explain a weakness."**

    Charming self-deprecation is good. But using your essay to make excuses for a low grade or another shortcoming usually just shines a light on the very thing you're trying deemphasize. It's like taking your shoes off at the beginning of a first date and saying, "Before this goes any further, I need to explain why my toenails are so grotesque." Some situations really do merit explanation, but most don't.

If you had an experience during your community service that really meant a lot to you, say so. And be honest. Otherwise, consider doing a good deed for admissions officers and avoid the community service cliché.

2. "Hard work always pays off," and other life lessons learned while playing sports

The problem with many sports essays is they explain what life is like for every athlete. You go to practice. You work hard. You compete.

Then the student makes it worse by saying sports taught him the importance of hard work and commitment, which is almost certainly not something he would say to his friends.

Be original. Tell your sports story that nobody else can tell. If you can't find a story you own, just write about something else. The sport will still be listed on your application.

3. "How my trip to another country broadened my horizons"

This essay essentially says, "France is very different from the United States—the food, the language, the customs. But I learned to appreciate the differences and to adapt to the ways of the French."

Visiting a country and noticing that it is different is not a story that you own. The admissions office doesn't want to read your travel journals. Instead, make yourself, not the country, the focus of the essay.

One of our students who had never previously ventured onto any sort of dance floor wrote that his trip to Spain was the first time he'd ever danced in front of other people. That wasn't an essay about how Spain was different—it was an essay about how he was different in Spain.

4. **"How I overcame a life challenge [that wasn't really all that challenging]"**

Essays can help admissions officers understand more about a student who has overcome legitimate hardship. But far too many other students misguidedly manufacture hardship in a college essay to try to gain sympathy or make excuses (e.g., for low grades). That won't work.

If you've had a difficult hardship and you want to talk about it, you should. Otherwise, it's probably better to choose a different topic. Note: The pet eulogy falls into this category. Lovely if you want to write one. Just don't include it as part of your college essay.

5. **Anything that doesn't really sound like you**

Your essays are supposed to give the readers a sense of your personality. So give your essays a sincerity test. Do they sound like you, or do they sound like you're trying to impress someone?

Don't use words you looked up in the thesaurus. There really is no place for "plethora" in a college essay. Don't quote Shakespeare or Plato or the Dali Lama unless that is really you. If your best friend reads it and says it sounds just like you, that's probably a good sign.

Sound like a teenager

When writing college essays, some students mysteriously transform themselves into aging philosophers. They mention how they were enchanted by lush scenery during their travels, how they experienced a profound epiphany during a volunteer shift at the homeless shelter, or the moment on the soccer field when a teammate was injured and they realized that soccer was, after all, just a game.

None of those stories sound like the teenagers who wrote them.

College essays aren't formal, academic pieces of writing like those you write in your English classes. College essays should sound like you, so the reader can figuratively hear your voice and get a sense for your personality. The admissions officers are trying to get to know you, and they don't expect you to think or sound like anything but a teenager. As the Brandeis University dean of admissions told The Boston Globe, "We expect people to write like seventeen- and eighteen-year-olds."[10]

We're not suggesting you should write your essays the same way you would text message a friend. I'm saying: relay the world the way you really see it. Colleges will find you much more charming if you're honest than they will if you try to be something you're not.

Here's a good way to strike the right tone without being too informal.

COMMITTEE NOTES

No McEssays

Ninety percent of the applications I read contain what I call McEssays— usually five-paragraph essays that consist primarily of abstractions and unsupported generalization. They are technically correct in that they are organized and have the correct sentence structure and spelling, but they are boring. Sort of like a Big Mac... If an essay starts out: "I have been a member of the band and it has taught me leadership, perseverance and hard work," I can almost recite the rest of the essay without reading it. Each of the three middle paragraphs gives a bit of support to an abstraction, and the final paragraph restates what has already been said. A McEssay is not wrong, but it is not going to be a positive factor in the admission decision. It will not allow a student to stand out.[9]

Parke Muth
Associate Dean of Admissions
University of Virginia

1. **For everything you write in your college essays, ask yourself, "Would I say this to someone else?"**

No athlete in the history of high school sports has ever said the words, "I personally feel very fortunate to have participated in varsity athletics because it has taught me the value of committing to my goals."

If you wouldn't say it to someone else, don't say it in your college essays. That will keep you from being too formal.

2. **Pretend you're telling your story to your favorite teacher.**

If you'd tell a story one way to your high school principal and another way to your best friend, your favorite teacher is probably the happy middle ground. Go to that middle ground when you're writing your college essays.

Too formal:

"I found chemistry to be a particularly challenging subject, as my natural academic strengths lie with writing."

Too informal:

"Chemistry blows. I'd pretty much rather do anything else than do even one problem set in chemistry."

Just right:

"Chemistry and I just don't get along. I don't know what it is about my brain, but it works a lot better when I'm reading Shakespeare than it does when I'm trying to memorize the periodic table."

Admit you're not perfect

Have you ever known someone who could admit when he wasn't good at something? Someone who laughed at herself easily? Or a person self-confident enough to own when he made a mistake? It's hard not to like those people. Since your college essay is all about helping the admissions officers like you, it doesn't hurt to occasionally poke a little fun at yourself.

Sometimes colleges ask essay questions about failures you've experienced or mistakes that you've made. Don't be afraid to answer those questions honestly. And never try to spin a positive as a negative, like, "Sometimes I can be too focused on my academics and can neglect time with my friends at the beach." That sounds like you're afraid to admit a real fault.

No successful person has been great at everything she's attempted. Admit you struggle in physics, you make the world's worst chocolate chip cookies, or no matter how hard you try, you can't paint a single image your classmates could identify. These things don't make you sound inferior—they make you sound human.

We're not suggesting you should write an entire essay about your failures or shortcomings. We're saying don't shy away from including those things when they're part of a topic you care about.

A kid who writes about working at a summer camp should absolutely share all the reasons he loved his job. But when he also mentions that the first night it was his turn to cook dinner, he undercooked all the hotdogs and none of the 40 campers would eat them, it makes him that much more likeable.

Admitting the occasional fault makes it easier to believe you when you claim to be really good at something. As long as you aren't admitting something that suggests you're a danger to yourself or others, doing so will probably help you get into college.

COMMITTEE NOTES

Admit a fault

I may be guilty of exaggerating, but the student I remember [most] quickly admitting a few years back was a young man who told us straight-out that after four years he was still the 'worst soccer player on the worst soccer team in the state.' Another who I remember saying to myself was someone who, when asked if there was anything else we should know, wrote, "As you will have noticed, my SAT scores are low. They are accurate."[11]

Fred Hargadon
Former Dean of Admissions
Princeton University

Seek feedback outside the family circle

A Collegewise student once brought us an essay in which he'd written that he struggled with "standardized testes." We're not kidding. Spell check doesn't catch everything, so it's a good idea to have a fellow human review your essay, too.

The best reviews are people you trust, and who actually know what they're doing. They should meet both criteria, not just one. For most students, your counselor and English teacher usually can. Friends, parents and friends of your parents usually can't.

Some parents are offended when they're told they shouldn't serve as their student's college essay advisors. They swear things are different in their families. Trust us, they're not. Your parents love you too much and are way too close to the subject matter to be impartial observers.

If your parents push you on this, show them the following excerpt from the American Medical Association's "Code of Medical Ethics," which advises against doctors treating their own children for similar reasons.

> Professional objectivity may be compromised when an immediate family member or the physician is the patient; the physician's personal feelings may unduly influence his or her professional medical judgment, thereby interfering with the care being delivered... If tensions develop in a physician's professional relationship with a family member, perhaps as a result of a negative medical outcome, such difficulties may be carried over into the family member's personal relationship with the physician.[12]

If a trained doctor should avoid diagnosing her daughter's flu-like symptoms, why should an untrained (or even trained) parent try to help her daughter with a college essay?

Take a proverbial page from the AMA and me here. Parents can and should be included in the college process with their kids. But the essays are one of those places where parents should step out and let someone else help.

Too much advice can hurt

Also, beware of seeking advice from too many people. When you shop around your essay for feedback, it can end up sounding like it was written by committee. When too many people give you too much advice, it just confuses you and leaves you unsure about what to write. "Don't let more than three people critique your essay. If you do, you'll get conflicting messages and your voice will be lost forever," advises Bryan Nance, former director of minority recruitment at MIT.[13]

Again, your English teacher and/or your counselor should be able to provide enough feedback. Everybody else—parents, uncles and siblings—can support you in other ways.

Rewrite before you reuse

Great stories for college essays tend to be recyclable. If your topic is something that really was important to you, you can apply that significance to a lot of college essay prompts.

But there's a difference between repurposing a story and reusing the exact same essay.

We once worked with a student who wrote an essay about how she had lost every high school election she'd ever run in. She wrote that each time she lost, she shrugged off the defeat and found another activity where she could be successful. It was a funny, self-deprecating peek into her personality, and it helped admissions officers get to know her better.

The student used the experience as the basis for great responses to several colleges' essay prompts:

> *"Describe a time when you failed or made a mistake. What did you learn from the experience?"*

> *"What is a talent, skill, activity, accomplishment or personal quality that makes you proud?"*

> *"How do you hope to contribute to our campus community?"*

> *"Describe a time when you faced a challenge or adversity."*

Each time she used the story, many of the details were the same, but she tailored the essay to answer the prompt. Those tailored versions addressed what each prompt asked for, and they were really well done—honest, engaging and focused.

When her real answer to a prompt had nothing to do with losing elections, she wrote different essays. But her "I am a good loser" theme worked for the essay prompts from more than half her colleges.

There's nothing wrong with recycling a story—especially if it does a great job answering the prompt. Just make sure you tailor it. Rewrite before you reuse.

Part V: How to Get Stronger Letters of Recommendation

Send only what they ask you to send

Many private colleges will ask you to submit letters of recommendation from teachers, counselors or people who know you personally. In most cases, you don't send these yourself; the writers send them directly to the school either by mail or electronically.

Colleges' applications will state very clearly how many letters they want (if they want any at all), and from whom they want them. A lot of the students want to ignore the instructions and send more letters than are requested. They include a letter from their dad's business partner who's an alumnus, even though the application clearly asks for letters from two teachers. Don't decide you're a special case who should ignore the instructions.

Martha C. Merrill, dean of admissions and financial aid at Connecticut College, offered another reason to submit exactly what's requested: "Admission officers will likely read only the required number of recommendations. If you submit too many, you leave it to chance which ones will be read."[14]

Personal beats famous

Some colleges also give you the opportunity to include a personal recommendation from a boss, coach, pastor, or someone else who knows you well. In those cases, the content of the letter is far more important than whether or not the person is famous or powerful. Asking the published author your mother treats at her medical practice to write a letter for you will not help your chances of admission if that author barely knows you.

Pay attention to each college's directions and send only what they ask you to send.

Choose the right teachers

Colleges have your transcript and your application, so they don't need a teacher to tell them what grade you earned in the class. They want the story behind the grades. Did you participate in class? Did you ask intelligent questions? Did you do reading outside of your English class, build a functioning greenhouse in biology or do an oral report in US history dressed up like George Washington?

To make sure you pick the right teachers to ask for letters of recommendation, consider the following questions:

1. What teachers have seen your very best work?

Don't just think about the grade you earned. In fact, your best work might have come in a class where you didn't necessarily earn an A, especially if it was particularly challenging and you still brought your best effort. Think about the projects you did, the questions you asked and the way you involved yourself in the class.

2. In which classes did you participate the most?

Where did you ask questions, contribute to class discussions or talk with the teacher outside of class about the subject matter?

3. In what classes did you find the material the most interesting?

Did the teacher know how interested you were? How? Did you talk with her after class, do additional reading or take on extra projects?

4. Which solid classes from your junior year fit the above criteria?

Unless a college requests something different, teacher letters of recommendation should come from solid subjects (e.g., math, English, science, social science or foreign language) that you took during your junior year. Why the junior year? It's the most recent full academic year from which to draw—the freshman and sophomore years are closer to ancient academic history.

COMMITTEE NOTES

It's not all about the grade

Teachers who gave you an A do not necessarily write better recs than those who gave you a lower grade. Students mature academically at different rates, and many colleges (including ours) are looking for students who are passionate about learning a tough subject, not necessarily those who are merely naturally talented.[15]

Evan Cudworth
Senior Assistant Director of Admissions
University of Chicago

Ask the right way

Some high schools have established systems for requesting letters of recommendation. They may establish deadlines or ask you to fill out a questionnaire to make the teacher or counselor's job easier. First, check with your counseling office and make sure you're following their instructions. Once you know the protocol, there's a right way—and a wrong way—to approach your teachers.

Many students make the mistake of stumbling up to a teacher at the end of class, dumping paperwork on his desk and asking if the teacher can write a letter of recommendation for an application that's due in two weeks. Not good.

Here's what we recommend:

- Ask early, preferably as early as possible in your senior year (once you have the necessary materials).
- Ask the teacher if you can make an appointment to talk about your college applications.
- When you ask, give the teacher some indication of why you are asking. For example,

"Mr. Trumbull, I'm applying to several small private colleges, and they recommend I find teachers who can comment on my participation and performance in their classes. I was wondering if you thought it would be appropriate for you to write me a strong letter of recommendation."

This is not only polite, but it also gently tells the teacher what you want him to say. It also gives the teacher an easy out. If he doesn't think he can write strongly about the characteristics you've described, he can say so, and you can move on to another teacher. Yes, it will sting a little bit, but it's better that you know and get the chance to ask someone else.

Waive your right

Each letter of recommendation form includes a portion you fill out before you give it to your teacher. It asks if you agree to waive your right to access the letter in the future.

If you waive your right, it means once the writer sends the letter to the school, you have no right to view it. You will never know what the writer said about you or whether it helped or hurt your chances of admission.

You should always waive your right.

Declining to waive your right essentially tells the writer that you don't trust him or her to do a good job, which is never a good strategy. Also, the college will wonder why you didn't feel comfortable enough to waive the right. It makes you look like you're hiding something.

If you feel uneasy about waiving your rights, consider asking someone else to write the letter, someone who's more unwaveringly positive about you.

If you're still uneasy, try to relax. Teachers and counselors are out to help, not hurt, students. Just about all of them will do their best to say something positive about a nice kid.

Once your teachers agree to write letters, make their jobs as easy as possible.

- Fill out the required student information at the top of each recommendation form.
- For each college, provide the teacher with an addressed, stamped envelope (use the admissions office's address as the return address).
- If the forms need to be submitted electronically, email the link to your teacher, or print it on a separate piece of paper.
- When you've got everything together, put the materials in one large envelope or folder for each school and give them your teacher.

Part VI: What to do after you submit

Resist letting fear hijack your applications

Your mind does terrible things to you before you make a big, irrevocable decision. Maybe that's why so many people are nervous on their wedding days? Before you hit "Submit," you'll second guess your essays. You'll wish your SAT scores were higher. You'll be embarrassed that you got a B in French or don't have more community service hours or only played varsity softball for one year. Don't worry. This is completely normal and almost always irrational.

The finality of submitting an application can be scary. You might have to deal with rejection. Or you might have to face the reality of leaving home and going someplace new. Taking any big step always comes with some nerves. That's normal. Once you expect it to happen, it's a lot less uncomfortable when it actually arrives.

On the other extreme, students sometimes let this fear hijack their college applications. They leave our offices with their applications reviewed and ready to submit, then return three or four weeks later and reveal that they haven't sent them. Waiting longer to take the last step doesn't seem to make these students any surer of themselves. They never edit and revise their way to a sense of comfort. The applications usually just get older, not better, during the delay.

The best way to diffuse this fear is to expect it. We're not trying to get all Dr. Phil on you, but you'll see what we mean once you're about to submit your applications. When a student is prepared for this spike in nerves, they're much less affected when it comes.

Give applications the time and attention they deserve. Then acknowledge that you've done your best and hit "Submit." The nerves will go away within a few days (maybe even in a few hours).

Bang a gong

Applying to college is a major milestone, and submitting your final application should be a celebration-worthy event. So take a cue from us and bang your own gong.

At one of the Collegewise office, when seniors submit their final college applications, they bang a two-foot gong right in the middle of the office. The gong sits on a custom-made metal stand with its accompanying mallet beneath a four-foot high "Rules of the Gong" poster, which specifies that it may only be banged by seniors who have submitted all of their applications.

In 2010 when we bought the gong, we were looking for a memorable way to let seniors celebrate their application completion. We suspected our students might think it was lame.

They actually love it.

We have yet to have one senior be too cool to bang the gong. As our former student, Silvie R., now at the University of Washington, said, "I was so proud of myself when I got to bang the gong in the Collegewise office when all of my applications were finished."

We love seeing the grins and looks of accomplishment on their faces. We all applaud and offer our congratulations. And their parents—who smartly step back and turn this process over to their students and Collegewise counselors—snap photos to capture their kids' gonging celebrations. A few moms have even joined their kids for their own photos in front of the gong. Kids have uploaded their gonging pictures to their Facebook pages.

Big, loud

For us, the gong is a big, loud acknowledgement of a job well done and a teenager taking one step closer to starting college. Most of them haven't yet received any admissions news, but that's no reason not to celebrate this important step. It reminds our students and parents that no matter which colleges say "Yes," they still have reason to be proud.

Don't delay your celebration for when decisions arrive. Bang your own gong. Celebrate the completion of your college applications in your own way. Do something else fun you've been too busy with applications to do. You don't need a college acceptance to do a little celebrating.

Make follow-up calls

When you submit a college application online, you usually get an online confirmation that it's been received. That doesn't necessarily mean the admissions committee has everything they need to consider your application complete. That's why it's a good idea to follow up with a phone call to each college a few weeks after you've submitted everything just to make sure they have what they need (and it's yet another reason to start the process early).

You aren't the only one contributing pieces of your college application. Testing agencies send test scores. Counselors send transcripts. Teachers send letters of recommendation. Colleges are absolutely inundated with materials at this time of year. It's easy for something to get lost in the shuffle.

Just call the admissions office (don't let your parents do this for you), tell them your name and that you recently submitted an application for admission, and ask if you can confirm that your application is complete. It's not rude to do this, and if they tell you they're missing something, don't panic. Just tell them you'll take care of it right away, and don't forget to thank them for their time. Remember: colleges are insanely busy during application season.

One follow-up phone call to each college can put your mind at ease and let you get on with your senior year.

Give thanks

Nobody gets into college alone. There are always supportive people in your corner who help you get there. So as you submit the last of your applications, take some time to thank the people who helped you.

Your high school counselor

Even if you never actually met to discuss your applications, counselors do a lot of work for you behind-the-scenes that you might not be aware of. They write school profiles that colleges request. They write letters of recommendation. They send transcripts and field phone calls and set up visits from college representatives.

Anyone who wrote your letters of recommendation

These people did you a favor and deserve to be thanked. It's also not unusual for a college to contact your counselor or one of your recommendation writers if they have a question about something that was unclear on your application. If that were to happen, what impression have you left? You wouldn't want your teacher to think, "He's the kid who asked me to write his letter 10 days before the deadline, gave me no supporting materials and never bothered to say thank you."

Write a note

One way to make your thanks especially meaningful is to write a note that shows you recognize they did a favor for you and that you sincerely appreciate the effort made on your behalf. Write it on stationery (not over email). Use proper grammar and punctuation. (Seriously, use proper grammar and punctuation.)

There's no formula for what to say. The key is to just be sincere and take the time to give a proper thanks. It makes a difference.

Dear Mr. Gerard:

Now that the college admissions process is officially over, I wanted to thank you again for taking the time to write my letters of recommendation. I can only imagine how many letters you must have written for students this fall. I know that most of my friends planned on asking you to write their letters, too. I really do appreciate the time and effort that you took for me.

I also wanted to tell you that I got accepted early decision to Hamilton College and I'm planning to major in history. I'm not sure I ever would have considered studying history in college if I hadn't taken your class, but after I did that oral report on the Hamilton-Burr duel in front of the entire class without passing out, I'm sure I'm ready for whatever college history throws my way.

You're a good teacher, Mr. Gerard, and I always looked forward to going to your class every day. My younger sister, Jenna, is a freshman this year, and I've told her to do whatever it takes to get into your class. She's a much better public speaker than I am, by the way, so she won't be prone to fainting when it's time to do oral reports.

I'm so excited to go to college, and I'm sure I would not have ended up where I did were it not for your help. Thank you again for everything you've done for me, and have a wonderful summer.

All my best,

Rebecca C.

Hamilton College Class of 2016

That's a student who took the time to give some sincere thanks.

While you're at it, don't forget to thank your parents. From providing moral support to paying for the SAT tutor, they likely deserve a healthy dose of your gratitude, too.

Anyone who provided emotional support, offered monetary support or just generally took an interest in your college quest and your happiness deserves to be thanked. It's so easy to say thank you, and you'd be surprised how often it comes back to you.

Resist the worries

You're done. You've submitted your applications, celebrated, followed up and thanked people. Now you have to wait to hear from colleges. So, exactly how much time should you spend worrying about it?

None, if you can swing it.

First of all, if you had your counselor approve your list, you're going to get in somewhere. If you did a thoughtful college search and found the right schools, that somewhere is bound to make you happy.

Worrying about whether or not your dream college is going to say "Yes" doesn't do you any good. It won't do a single thing to influence the result. We suggest you resist the urge.

COMMITTEE NOTES

Stay focused after submitting

You have work to get through in the next few months and it's going to prepare you for the next step, which isn't going to be any easier. Besides that, worrying about an application that is already submitted isn't going to affect the outcome and it's apt to take you away from those pressing academic tasks. [16]

University of Virginia
Office of Undergraduate Admissions blog

In our experience, the happiest students accept that what happens from here is out of their hands. They'll spend their time dreaming about how great college is going to be, how much they're going to learn and how much fun they're going to have no matter where they go.

They also keep in perspective that nobody's life is made or broken by an admissions decision from a particular college. If a school you love denies you, you're still going to college. You're still going make new friends and have four years of fun and learning no matter where you go. You have so much to look forward to; it just doesn't make sense to worry.

Keep up the good work

"Keep your grades up" often sounds like one of those empty platitudes adults say to seniors who've applied to college. In fact, doing so really can make a difference where you get in.

Most private colleges, as well as public schools like the University of Michigan, will ask you to send a seventh semester transcript (also called a "Mid-Year Report") once you complete the first semester of your senior year. Those grades will be reviewed before the school makes a decision.

Also, if you get wait-listed by a college, they might ask to see your second semester grades from senior year. Since students often aren't taken off waiting lists until after they graduate from high school, those colleges have the opportunity to look at your entire senior year's academic work before they make a decision.

Students who are taking Advanced Placement or International Baccalaureate courses, who keep up the good work and score well on their associated exams, can also end up with college credit. That can let you skip certain introductory classes your freshman year and maybe even graduate from college early.

Finally, every college will ask you to send a complete transcript once you're admitted. They'll look at both semesters of your senior year to make sure that you finished the classes you told them you were taking and that you kept doing as well as you'd done in the previous years. If you haven't kept up the good work, they can rescind your offer of admission.

Senior party

Some students let the senior party start too early. Even straight-A students who end up getting a couple C's or a D in their senior year can lose their admission to their

usually take place on campus and can be a great way to learn more about a school you're really interested in without the added pressure of admissions judgment. As Carleton College's website advises for students scheduling interviews: "Relax. Interviews are informational, not evaluative. We're not making black marks against you on a checklist. The goal is just to get better acquainted."[5]

If you'd be excited to learn more about the school from someone who can really answer your questions, great. But don't schedule an informative interview just because you think you should.

Our Collegewise counselor Arun, conducted informative interviews as an assistant director of admissions at The University of Chicago and painfully recalls the awkward silences when a student knew seemingly nothing about the school and had no questions. In one of his better experiences, the student looked past him and said, "Hey, what books are those on your shelf?" They spent the next 30 minutes talking about their favorite authors.

"Evaluative interviews," on the other hand, mean that what you say can and will be used to judge you in the court of admissions. Colleges may offer them on campus with admissions officers or current students, locally with volunteer alumni who live near the applicants, or both.

Most colleges' websites will tell you whether their interviews are informative or evaluative. For example, Yale's website clearly states: "All Yale interviews, both those with alumni and those with current Yale seniors, are evaluative. We read interview reports along with all your other application materials."[6]

Claremont McKenna College's site says: "Interviews at CMC are informational in nature, not evaluative. You should expect to get answers to any questions you may have about CMC or the admission process."[7]

3. Does the college recommend that you interview?

Colleges express varying levels of desire to have prospective students interview. Some take a decision not to interview as a sign you're not that interested in the school. Others have no preference. Once again, most will make their feelings clear on their websites. Five examples:

Pomona College

> "Southern California applicants are expected to interview and must do so on campus."

Wake Forest University

"Interviews are strongly recommended for first-year applicants."

Oberlin College

"Interviews are not required for admission, except in the case of homeschooled students and students graduating from high school in less than four years. We do recommend interviews for all applicants visiting campus."

Reed College

"Interviews are not required for application to Reed, and you will not be at a disadvantage in the admission process if you do not schedule one."

University of Pennsylvania

"Not having an interview will not be held against you. Since interviews are not required nor are they offered to all applicants at this time, we encourage you to rely upon your application for admission as a forum for presenting the many unique aspects of your candidacy."

Again: visit the colleges' websites to get the interview scoop. A college guide-book might tell you an interview is "not required for admission," but you can see from this limited sampling it's not always that cut-and-dried.

4. How are interviews scheduled?

On-campus interviews usually need to be scheduled ahead of time. The schools' websites will tell you when interviews are offered and how to schedule one.

The opportunity to interview with local alumni usually depends on whether a volunteer interviewer lives in your area. Most alumni interviews take place at a mutually convenient location, like a coffee shop or at the interviewer's workplace. Some colleges require that students request these interviews. Many other schools simply tell students once they submit their application, they'll be contacted by an interviewer if one lives in their area.

Bottom line: Before you buy a plane ticket or get your nice clothes pressed, find out the answers to these questions. And rely only on the colleges' own websites to get them.

Make conversation

Students who get nervous before their college interviews are usually worried that, like a job interview, their most important objective is to give the right answers. Instead of relaxing and having an interesting conversation with their interviewer, they sit there passively waiting to be asked questions, then trying to give what they hope are the right answers—all the while appearing like they're on the verge of cardiac arrest.

This is not a job interview. Your college interviewers don't have prepared questions in hand, and they aren't looking for you to give the right answers. The interviewer's goal is to get to know you and see if you can have a good conversation with an adult.

John Detore, an alumni interviewer for MIT, offered this interview advice on the school's admissions blog: "I've talked to lots of candidates and the ones who are just themselves, who can laugh at their mistakes and struggles, who seem comfortable in their own skin—inevitably show a bit more maturity, and inevitably make the best impression. Just my two cents."[8]

There's something likeable about a teenager who's confident and mature enough to sit comfortably with an adult and chat about a variety of topics. They smile easily, tell good stories and ask good questions. And most importantly, they're not afraid to admit what they aren't good at or what they don't know. That's why it's so important to understand that this is much more a conversation than it is a test to see if you can give the right answers.

If you can be that mature and comfortable with your college interviewer, it's a sign that you'll be able to do the same thing when meeting with your professors and your academic advisor in college. Your answers aren't being scored by a panel of judges. The best thing an interviewer could say about you is that you're an interesting student that he or she enjoyed meeting and talking with.

Goes both ways

Remember: good conversation goes both ways. Have you ever been on a first date with someone who was a terrible conversationalist and made you do all the talking? It's just about the most agonizing thing in the world. You sit there trying desperately to think of things to say so you can avoid the excruciating silence that you know is going to come unless you keep talking. After about 20 minutes of trying, you want to pull an imaginary ejection handle and catapult yourself out of there.

If you sit in your college interview waiting to be asked questions and then give short answers without any details, it's like putting the interviewer through a terrible first date. That leads to exchanges like this:

Interviewer: "Can you tell me about playing violin in the orchestra?"

"Yes. I am a first chair violinist in my school orchestra and I take lessons five hours every week."

A brief answer like that puts all the effort of conversation on your interviewer. What if this student had thought ahead of time what he might like to say about orchestra and given a more thoughtful response, like:

"Sure. My mom played the violin growing up and she really encouraged me to join my school's orchestra program when I was in sixth grade. I've been playing ever since. Sometimes it's been a little rough being the only guy at my high school who plays the violin, but I'm glad I stuck with it. Last year, my school's orchestra actually traveled to Amsterdam to play. It was the first time I'd ever been out of the country, so that was pretty great."

Rather than sounding like a line from a resume, the second response tells a quick story and made some interesting conversation. It gives the interviewer the chance to follow up with another question, like what it's like to be the only guy at school who plays the violin, or what you thought of Amsterdam, or whether or not you and your mom have bonded over the violin.

If you want to be impressive, make the interviewer's job easier. Give some detail to your answers and tell a story. Be a good conversationalist. Don't just sit there.

Respond promptly when contacted

If your target college requests an alumni interview, your interviewer will likely reach out to you by phone or email after you apply. When they do, it's important to respond promptly.

We've heard several college interviewers tell stories about leaving voicemails or sending emails to kids who don't respond for four to five days. That makes it much harder for them to schedule with you and doesn't send a very good message about your interest.

You don't have to be on high alert and respond within 15 minutes of being contacted. But during the college admissions process, it's a good idea to check to shop before the interview actually starts. This can be a potentially awkward walk of silence for a student that's not prepared. When you start the walk, initiate the conversation with something like, "Thanks so much for seeing me today," or "So, how many interviews do you have scheduled today?"

In just the first five seconds, you'll have shown your interviewer that you're confident, mature and a good conversationalist.

Make a good last impression

Parents often nag kids to write thank-you notes to their college interviewers. This is one of those times when your parents are right.

Your college interviewer has already been to college and doesn't need anything from you. They're giving up time for you and they deserve to be thanked. Our Collegewise counselor Arun recommends students send an email, not an old-fashioned card. "Cards get thrown away. An email gets printed and added to their folder," he says.

If your interviewer hasn't previously communicated with you over email, ask for his or her card at the end of the interview. And remember the laws of capitalization and punctuation are not suspended just because it's email. If you can't get an email address, go the old-fashioned route and write a thank-you card. Whichever route you choose, make the note a good one.

Not all thank-you notes are created equal. Some are only two or three sentences and sound like they were written by a corporation. They're the thank-you version of "We apologize for any inconvenience."

As covered in "Give thanks," good thank-you notes are sincere. This person gave up time for you and deserves to be thanked. Sound like a real human. And specifically reference something about the interview that was helpful or interesting to you, even if it wasn't relevant.

A student who writes, "I'm also glad to learn I'm not the only one who thinks Arrested Development was the greatest show in television history!" wouldn't just personalize the note, it also would remind the interviewer of the conversation and the student—you.

Finally, send your email or write your card the day after the interview. You don't know how many students your interviewer is seeing after you, and if you wait a couple weeks to send your thank you, your name and face might be figuratively fuzzy. 🎓

7.

Affording College:

How to Get Financial Aid and Scholarships

 Since we used one of the FAFSA estimation calculators, *we knew with two high tech incomes that we wouldn't qualify for any need-based financial aid. Because our son has excellent grades and test scores, we made sure that some of the colleges on his list were reputed to give good merit scholarships. Chapman University offered him a $25,000 per year presidential scholarship, bringing the total close to in-state costs at a University of California campus. It was also a great boost to my son's confidence that his hard work was paying off—it's not every day someone offers you $100,000 to go to college. Even University of California—Berkeley where he enrolled offered us unsubsidized loans for the full cost of attendance.*

Lynn C.
Mother of Noah K., former Collegewise student,
Class of 2012
University of California—Berkeley

It's going to take a couple cycles to see just how effective the net price calculator is. But college financial aid had long needed to be reengineered so families didn't have to apply and just cross their fingers with no idea whether or not they'd qualify for aid. The net price calculator is a good first step.

Be as accurate as you can when inputting the numbers. If you and your parents decide to change your college list based on the results, ask your high school counselor if she can recommend some schools that would be appropriate.

Look beyond sticker price

We naturally make decisions about whether we can afford things based on how much they cost. That makes it easy to tell what's in—and out—of our price range. But paying for college works differently.

The Free Application for Federal Student Aid (FAFSA)—which you file in January of the year you plan to start college—is the starting point for applying for aid for any four-year college.

When you file the FAFSA, the figure the government returns to you is your Expected Family Contribution (EFC). That's the amount your family will be expected to pay for the upcoming year at any college. It will be up to the government and the colleges to come up with a financial aid package (that may include loans that will need to be paid back) to make up the difference between your EFC and the full cost of attendance at each school.

For example, if your EFC is $20,000, and you apply to a school that costs $30,000 a year to attend, you've demonstrated $10,000 in financial need.

So in theory, whether a school costs $10,000 a year or $50,000 a year, you will pay the same EFC amount at the time of enrollment at each school—$20,000 using the example above. That's what you've demonstrated you can afford.

There's more

We say "in theory" because about 270 private schools believe that the FAFSA doesn't tell them enough about your ability to pay. They may require you to fill out additional forms that enable them to calculate their own EFC, and that number can be higher or lower than the number the FAFSA gives you. Still, using the aforementioned net price calculator removes a lot of that guesswork.

Of course, the amount of aid you can receive isn't dependent only on how much money you have (or don't have). Your academic strength, match with the school, and the college's desire to have you on campus can also influence a financial aid award.

We don't recommend applying to a list of schools that are all out of your price range. But since you're dealing with estimates, never cross a school off your list just because it exceeds a certain sticker price.

PARENT TO PARENT

Kami was awarded grants, academic scholarships and performance scholarships from all of the colleges she applied to—everything Collegewise told us about not letting the price tag of some colleges scare you off. You never know what they will award you!

Kim K.
Mother of Kami, former Collegewise student, Class of 2012
Point Loma Nazerene University

Never Pay to Complete the FAFSA

"F" is for Free

Use only the official FAFSA website, http://www.fafsa.ed.gov/, where you can complete the form free of charge. Typing "FAFSA" into a search engine will bring up services that charge you to complete it.

Apply the admissions advice

Applying for financial aid is a totally different process than applying for admission. There are different forms with different deadlines, all of which are handled by an entirely different office on college campuses. But our advice about applying for admission is exactly the same when applying for financial aid: Start early, find out what's required, and follow the directions.

The only guaranteed, mistake-free way to make sure you file the correct forms by the deadlines is to visit the financial aid section of each college's website and verify what they require. That's your first step. In the fall of your senior year, visit the financial aid sections of your colleges' websites and find the answers to three crucial questions:

1. What forms do you need to fill out to apply for need-based financial aid (e.g., Free Application for Federal Student Aid, school-specific forms, etc.)?

2. Do the financial aid offices require any supporting documentation? For example, some colleges require information from stepparents, or parents' income tax returns or business statements.

3. What are the deadlines to submit all of those required forms?

Narrow window

You'll notice many of the deadlines fall between January and March of the senior year, and many of the forms you need to fill out can't actually be started until after January 1. It takes time to gather all this information and January to March is a narrow window to complete everything that's required. Even if you can't officially start filling out forms now, you can at least set yourself up to finish everything as early as possible once the filing window opens.

Get a Jump on the FAFSA

Each October, The Princeton Review publishes an updated edition of our book *Paying for College Without Going Broke*. It includes a sample FAFSA for the upcoming year as well as a ton of advice from Kalman Chany, a consultant who has helped thousands of families navigate the financial aid process as well as led workshops and trainings on that process for corporations, schools, and financial professionals. You still won't be able to complete the real FAFSA until the following January, but completing our sample is like a FAFSA practice run for parents who would like one.

Just like when you fill out college applications, always follow directions. Send colleges what they ask for, when they ask for it. You aren't the one to decide that your situation necessitates a better way. If you have questions, contact the college's office of financial aid directly.

Talk to your parents about costs

A lot of parents believe they should shield their kids from the economic realities of attending college—that it's your job to get accepted and their job to pay for it. While that is an honorable view, it's good for students to have honest, open discussions with their parents about college costs.

It's not unreasonable for a student to know what her parents can afford to pay for college, the sacrifices they've made to save or the continued sacrifices they'll make during the four years they have to write tuition checks. Having that conversation now, however unpleasant it might be, is much better than having it later, when you have an offer of admission in hand, but your family can't afford the school.

Says Kate P., a class of 2012 Collegewise student who went on to the University of Arizona: "I'm glad my parents shared our financial abilities with me because it helped me realize that some of my schools were very unrealistic. Knowing what my family was able to sacrifice to send me to college helped me choose schools that I knew were affordable."

Financial aid impact

Even a student who isn't aware of his family's finances might be impacted when applying for financial aid. Not all financial aid is free money. Sometimes it includes loans, and those loans will be taken out in your name, even if your parents pay your tuition. That means you'll be legally obligated to start paying back that money (once you graduate from college).

Another type of financial aid is "work study," where you're offered a part-time job on campus to help defray college costs. You—not your parents—will be the one washing dishes, manning the front desk of the library or filing papers in the dean of student's office. That's why college financing is often a family decision, whether your parents want it that way or not.

If you're mature enough to go to college, you're mature enough to know what it'll take to pay for it. So even if your parents haven't brought it up, talk to them about college costs. Ask them if they'd be willing to share that information with you. Even if they insist on keeping it secret, you'll at least have given them one more example that you're taking this seriously and that you appreciate everything they're doing to send you to college.

Apply to colleges that may pay

Financial aid isn't all cold, hard numbers measuring costs and what your family can afford to pay. Financial aid offices have a lot of power to offer more generous packages to students they think are right for the school and are more likely to attend. That's why one of the best ways to get more financial aid is to apply to plenty of "target" and "safety" schools (see "How to Finalize Your List").

At a minimum, most colleges will offer you the financial aid you qualify for. But the specific aid package you're offered, and whether or not that package is even more generous than what you're eligible for, can have a lot to do with how badly the admissions office wants you at that school.

If you're a strong student who fits well with that college, the financial aid office may give you an award package that has more free money, with fewer loans or work-study components.

If they're not as interested in you, the opposite might be true.

If a school really wants you, they also can give you a scholarship that has absolutely nothing to do with financial need.

Financial aid offices earmark a certain percentage of money every year just to lure academically appealing students. This practice is called preferential packaging, and it's not a dirty secret. Note the following from the financial aid office at Muhlenberg College in Allentown, Penn.:

> Preferential packaging means, simply, that the students a college would most like to enroll will receive the most advantageous financial aid packages. A preferential financial aid package includes a far greater percentage of grant aid than self-help (loans and work). Because they have discretion over how much grant aid they choose to award a student, a college can award a bigger grant to a student they would really like to enroll. In some cases, the total of grant from the college and the loans the student is entitled to may exceed the student's financial need.[3]

Rule of thumb

The simple rule of thumb: if you want more financial aid, apply to the schools most likely to accept you.

Every year, we have B and even C students at Collegewise who get generous and unsolicited offers of aid from colleges. They do it by applying to plenty of target and safety schools that fit them well, and where they have a good chance of being admitted. The better the fit between you and a college, the more likely that school will entice you to attend.

Regardless of your GPA, you can find target and safety schools and avail yourself of potential scholarships. One former Collegewise student with a 2.8 GPA and an 18 on the ACT got a $6,000-per-year merit-based scholarship from Westminster College in Salt Lake City, Utah.

Find a financial safety school, too

We also recommend that you pick a financial safety school, one you're sure you can get into and pay for even if you get no financial aid.

If you apply to the right colleges, use the net price calculator and file all the appropriate forms, you probably won't need a financial safety school. Still, it's always good to have a fallback position when things don't go as planned. If there's one thing families have learned since the U.S. economy collapsed in 2008, it's how fast our family financial situations can change for the worse.

If you're not sure there are any schools you could afford without financial aid, take a look at the public universities in your state, ask your counselor which ones you have the best chance of being admitted to and make one your financial safety school.

Remember, nobody is saying you necessarily have to go to your financial safety school. But it's much better to at least have the option if things don't work out as you expected them to.

Update schools if circumstances change

When you file your financial aid forms, you give the colleges a financial snapshot of your family. If the snapshot changes before you get your financial aid award, it's important to update schools so they have the most recent information.

Financial aid offices want to know if there's a significant change to the information you shared on your forms. If your parent loses a job, or your family has unforeseen medical expenses, or your parents get divorced, all of those things impact how much your family can afford to pay for college. All of them are worth sharing with the financial aid office.

If you're not sure whether a change is substantial enough to share, update the school anyway. The worst thing that can happen is that the school doesn't use the information.

Compare awards

A lot of families get swept up by the total figure in the financial aid award letter.

When a college says you've been awarded $16,000 in financial aid, the figure sounds great. But it doesn't necessarily mean you're getting a $16,000 discount off the college's sticker price.

Financial aid awards can be a combination of free money (scholarships), loans and work study. To figure out who's giving you the best offer, you need to consider the total cost of attendance for the college, the amount of free money, the amount of the loans and accompanying interest rates. It's a challenging project even for someone who loves math and spreadsheets—and there's an easier way.

Visit www.finaid.org and use their Award Comparison Tools. http://www.finaid.org/You plug in the numbers for each school—the cost of attendance, the amounts of the scholarships, loans and work study. They'll give you the bottom-line figure of how much each school will cost.

You may or may not decide to pick your college based just on the price. But no matter how much you plan to factor cost into your final choice, compare your award letters so you know the real cost of each school.

Tell colleges about better offers

If you receive two very different offers of aid from two different schools, consider calling the college that gave you less aid and asking if there is any way they will reevaluate your package.

Families have often heard that you can leverage one financial aid offer into a more attractive offer from another school; that if you call a school and point out that another college is giving you a lot more money, you can almost negotiate your way to a higher package.

That scenario doesn't always pan out. You're not buying a used car here. Financial aid officers aren't likely to do anything that feels like haggling.

But we've seen it work. There are times when making that call can lead to a good outcome, especially if the two schools compete for the same applicants, and if the offers are very different.

Here are two things to keep in mind when making such a call.

1. Financial aid officers have an unstated sense of a collegiate pecking order. If you call a prestigious school that rejects most its applicants and tell them you've been awarded a more generous aid package from a school they've never heard of, they won't likely be inclined to give you more money. We're not saying you shouldn't ask, but know your argument will have less oomph.

2. Approach this like a civil business discussion. Leave your emotions out of it. Be polite and respectful. If there are substantial differences between the two awards, the college will probably ask to see a copy of the other award. Offer to provide any additional documentation that might be helpful. And always thank the person no matter what the outcome.

Enlist your parents

This is an appropriate call for a parent—not the student—to make. Students should always make contact with colleges themselves, but when it's time to discuss how to pay the bill, colleges expect the majority of those calls will come from parents.

Paying for college is a big deal and you want to know you've done everything you can do to get the aid you qualify for. So don't get your hopes up that you'll somehow negotiate your way to a higher aid package. Don't hesitate to call and ask, either.

Answer the $2,800 question

At Collegewise, we meet a lot of families who have the impression there is oodles of money available from outside or private scholarships. These are little-known awards from private companies, foundations, community organizations, churches, and other benefactors. There is money to be had from those sources, and they may be worth applying for, but you won't likely get a free ride from outside scholarships alone.

According to *Paying for College Without Going Broke*, the money from outside scholarships accounts for only about 5 percent of the aid that is available. Chany points out the biggest chunk of scholarship money comes from funds provided by the federal and state governments, and from the colleges themselves, all of which you access by following each college's directions to apply for financial aid.

That said, and even if the amount of money available from outside scholarships is comparatively small, free money for college is always a good thing. So here's how we recommend families go about deciding whether or not to apply: consider the time investment.

Survey says

In 2008, the National Postsecondary Student Aid Study surveyed 140,000 undergraduate students about how they paid for college. Among students enrolled full time at four-year colleges, 10.6 percent received scholarships. So the odds of winning a scholarship for students pursuing a bachelor's degree are about 1 in 10.[4] The average award was roughly $2,800.

Applying for outside scholarships is a time-consuming process. Kids have to research and find the scholarships, fill out the applications, and often write essays, get additional letters of recommendation and maybe even interview. If you devoted 10 to 15 hours of work to win $2,800, would you think it was worth it?

If your answer is, "Of course!" apply for outside scholarships.

If you'd feel like a $2,800 return on your investment of time and energy just wouldn't be worth it, you might reconsider.

Of course, that figure is an approximation. You could win more or less than $2,800, depending on your qualifications. The experience of our Collegewise students has supported the logic in *Paying for College Without Going Broke*; the biggest awards don't come from the outside scholarships. We can't recall ever hearing one of our students won a $15,000 scholarship from a private foundation or company. We see it happen all the time from the other sources, particularly from the colleges themselves.

If you decide to search for outside scholarships, all the information is available free to you. Two of the best places to search: www.scholarships.com and www. fastweb.com. 🎓

8.

Deciding:

How to Handle
Admissions Decisions
and Pick Your College

We did acknowledge each acceptance with high fives and congratulations on the specifics. "Wow! You got invited to apply for honors." "Just think about the great snowboarding." "That $5,000 scholarship will really help." "Getting the Presidential Scholarship must mean they really want you." When the last notice came in, we went out to dinner to celebrate all of them. And when his decision was made, we immediately placed a web order for a college logo sweatshirt so he could wear it at admitted students' day.

Lynn C.
Mother of Noah K., former Collegewise student,
Class of 2012
University of California—Berkeley

CHAPTER 8

Deciding:

How to Handle Admissions Decisions and Pick Your College

Celebrate every offer of admission

As acceptances start to roll in, some seniors hold off their excitement until the dream school's decision arrives.

We say, celebrate every offer of admission. It doesn't matter if it's your safety school. You're going to college.

As soon as you get more than one acceptance, you'll get to pick which college you want to attend. Whether you get three or five or 12 acceptances, life is good. Be proud that you worked hard enough to earn this, and enjoy the process of deciding where you're going to spend the next four years.

Make rejection pain temporary

It's never a great day when bad news arrives from a college. If this news comes from one of your dream schools, it's pretty disappointing. We can only offer that like bad hair cuts and bad break-ups, the pain will eventually pass.

You are allowed to be disappointed by a rejection. But (warning, a little tough love coming here), you are not allowed to treat the rejection like a tragedy.

This isn't a tragedy; it's a disappointment, and all successful people have their share of them. It's important to remember how lucky you are to be living in a country with the best system of higher education in the world. Wherever you go, you will carve out a college experience that you'll one day tell your kids about. It's still going to happen, and that's something worth appreciating.

College rejections often feel bitterly personal. But a rejection does not necessarily mean the admissions office didn't love your essay or appreciate your activities or think you wouldn't be a great addition to the campus.

HOW THEY CELEBRATED

Our Collegewise families celebrate every offer of admission. Here's how a few of them did it.

Collegewise Student	College attended	How they celebrated each acceptance
Noah K.	UC Berkeley	Noah's family gave each other group high fives as each decision arrived, and enjoyed a family dinner out to celebrate his choices at the culmination of the process.
Mike A.	Syracuse University	Mike's parents sent an email to their extended family around the country as each acceptance arrived (even for the safety schools).
Aaron F.	Southern Methodist University	When each acceptance arrived, Aaron's mother bought two Mylar balloons in the school colors to display in their house. When the next acceptance arrived, new balloons were added to the others. Soon there was a giant bouquet of balloons in the kitchen.
Lizzie H.	University of Arizona	For each acceptance, Lizzie's mother baked a cake frosted in the school's colors.

"The truth is that there is always a reason that colleges accept a student, but very often there is not a reason that they don't," writes A. Lucido, vice provost for enrollment policy and management at the University of Southern California. "It's truly nothing you did—or even didn't do… There are many more applicants than spaces in the class at selective universities, and we cannot take all the students that we would love to have on our campuses."[1]

Look ahead

One of the best ways to get over a college rejection is to look ahead six months from now.

You'll move into a dorm. You'll meet your new roommate while your parents exact your promise to call home on a regular basis. You'll buy a sweatshirt bearing the name of your new college. You'll go to your first college class, start making your new friends and officially begin your life as a college freshman.

Do you have any idea just how exciting that's going to be for you?

When we reach out to our former students who are in college, the overwhelming majority are blissfully happy where they are, regardless of whether they're attending what was once their first-choice school. Can you blame them? Have you ever been to a college party? Have faith that you'll be happy, too.

Six months from now, the college rejection that stings today will be a distant memory. So you're allowed a brief period of mourning if necessary. But as quickly as you can, move on. The sooner you begin falling in love with a college (if you're not already) that said, "Yes," the sooner you'll be excited about the next four years.

"I didn't get into my number one choice and now I can't believe I wanted to go somewhere else besides SMU," says former Collegewise student Taylor O. "College is literally the best thing that's happened to me and I can't see myself anywhere besides the place I ended up. I can't believe I am almost done with my first year here. I wish I could go back and start all over again."

Resist the urge to appeal

An appeal is a formal request you send in writing, asking a college to reconsider your application for admission. We've met students whose knee-jerk reaction to a rejection is to appeal as a way of not taking "No" for an answer. In most cases, that's like asking for a second opinion from the same doctor who's already diagnosed you, which is why we rarely see appeals work.

Those few cases where an appeal has led to an admission is when a student provides new and compelling information that wasn't originally in the application. For example, if your seventh semester grades were a dramatic improvement over your previous grades, or a club you started raised a large amount of money for a charity event you planned, or the new internship you just secured happens to be in the field you plan on majoring in, these are things that can be taken into account when reconsidering your application. None of these scenarios mean a college will necessarily overturn their decision, but at least you're presenting new information.

Some students want to appeal a decision because they simply believe they are stronger applicants than other students from their school who were admitted. Colleges won't consider this a valid reason to overturn their original decision. Don't point out the reasons you think you deserve the admission more than other students did. That just makes you look bitter.

Read and research

If you decide you want to appeal, carefully read the decision letter the college sent you, and research the admissions section of the college's website to see if any information about appealing decisions is provided. Then write a letter as soon as possible explaining why you want the admissions committee to reconsider your application for admission. Be polite and respectful, and make sure to present new information. If the college indicates extra letters of recommendation will be accepted in appeals cases, consider asking a teacher to write a letter of recommendation (a different teacher than you asked before).

It's disappointing not to be accepted to a school you really wanted to attend, but you'll be able to move past the disappointment faster if you let yourself start getting excited about your other colleges.

Unless you have new information the college didn't have when you submitted your application, resist the urge to appeal and start moving on.

Consider declining the waiting-list spot

Instead of receiving an acceptance or a rejection from a college, some students are offered a waiting-list spot and told they might be admitted later if more space becomes available.

It's the college admissions version of purgatory.

Colleges don't know how many accepted students will ultimately decide to enroll. A waiting list is a school's way of hedging its bets and making sure their freshman class is ultimately full.

Waiting lists help schools but create a lot of stress for the students placed on them. That's why I tell every student offered a spot on a waiting list to seriously consider saying, "No thanks."

A spot on a waiting list makes your college future uncertain. You don't know if you'll be taken off the list, and the statistics aren't encouraging. The National Association for College Admissions Counseling reported that nearly half of all colleges used waiting lists in 2010, but only 28 percent of wait-listed students were ultimately admitted (the most selective colleges admitted only 11 percent).[2]

It's also quite common for schools to have little or no financial aid left for students admitted off the waiting list. The University of San Diego's website says, "Typically, there is no financial aid available to students admitted from the waitlist."

Meanwhile, by May 1, you still have to commit to another college that accepted you. I've seen students make their commitment to a school but refrain from buying a sweatshirt or otherwise celebrating because they were still holding out hope to be admitted from another school's waiting list.

Again: college admissions purgatory.

No thanks

Your alternative is to say, "No thanks."

A student who declines a spot on a waiting list takes control of his college destiny. Instead of hoping for a change in his waiting-list status, he can focus on real options that are available to him and plan visits to schools he knows he could attend. He can compare offers from schools that gave him financial aid, commit to a college that's ready to commit to him and know where he's going to school in the fall.

It wasn't your choice to get a wait-list decision, but it's your choice whether or not you want to keep your spot on it.

Don't decline a waiting-list offer rashly, and don't do so without talking it over with your parents and counselor. Just remember you're in charge. You aren't obligated to accept a spot on a waiting list. There's no shame in deciding to attend a college that accepted you outright.

Accept an offer

We can't overemphasize the importance of accepting an offer of admission by May 1, "Decision Day," from one of the colleges that accepted you. The fact you're on a waiting list someplace else doesn't mean the colleges who said "Yes" will hold a spot. So even if you're holding out hope for a waiting-list school, commit by May 1 to another college.

When you officially do commit, allow yourself to be excited. At least one school you've picked said, "Yes."

They didn't need to wait to see who else enrolled before they admitted you. They deserve some excitement, and so do you. Make an emotional commitment to your new school and keep the waiting-list school as your back-up plan.

Improve your odds

If the school that wait-listed you really is your top choice and you want to pursue the option, the best way to improve your odds is to make contact with an admissions officer and express your desire to attend.

1. **Call the admissions office.**

Since admissions officers will rarely tell you something specific kept you from being admitted, the purpose of this phone call is primarily to show the admissions officer your level of maturity and your sincere interest in attending the school.

Explain you intend to accept the offer to be placed on the waiting list, and you are calling to find out if there might be anything specific you could address that would improve your chances of admission.

Before you hang up, write down the person's name (you're going to write a letter to him or her next).

2. **Meet with your counselor.**

It's also a good idea to meet with your high school counselor and tell her about your waiting-list situation.

If you've followed the advice in this book (you've already established a relationship with your counselor and you asked her to approve your college list), you can ask her if she would call the admissions office on your behalf to see what you can do. Admissions officers can sometimes be more candid with a counselor than they can be with a student.

3. **Write a letter.**

Many admissions officers tell me they are instructed to only pull kids off the waiting list who have made the effort to express their interest in the school. They don't want to pull kids off the waiting list who aren't really interested.

Your letter can be just two or three paragraphs. Thank them for taking the time to speak with you, update them on any recent achievements or awards you've earned since applying and reiterate your interest in the school.

If the school is your first choice (and it really should be if you're accepting a spot on the waiting list), make that clear in the letter.

SAMPLE WAITING LIST FOLLOW-UP LETTER

Below is a sample letter from a wait-listed student to an admissions officer at a college they are hoping to attend. This letter is something you want the admissions office to have in their office by the third week of April. Do not copy what you see below. Use it as a guideline. In order make the effective impression on the admissions officer, you need to be honest and specific with your reasons. Don't just copy from their viewbook or website, either. Being genuine and enthusiastic goes a long way with admissions officers.

Name of admissions officer you've spoken with
Title
Name of college
College's address
City, State, Zip code

Dear Mr. Burns,

Thank you for taking the time to speak with me last week about my status on the waiting list. While I was disappointed, I'm still excited about the possibility of attending this fall. When I first visited the University of Pennsylvania last summer, I made the smart decision and sat in Professor Hibberts' introductory vertebrate biology class and really enjoyed the discussion that took place. I also

The opening paragraph should thank them for taking the time to speak with you (be specific and mention the date you spoke on the phone) and explain that you are sending this letter to update the office on your progress. Feel free to express your disappointment at not being accepted, but keep the tone upbeat and optimistic as you share why you want to attend this college.

appreciated the balance Penn students I met in the student union showed with their academics and activities. I love the fact that I can work hard as a biology student and still enjoy supporting a competitive basketball team and study abroad at the Barcelona campus.

Since I submitted my application in December, there have been some updates to my academic and extracurricular record.

- In the most rigorous program of study available at Springfield High School, I received four A's in AP courses (including AP physics) and one B in honors calculus in the 3rd quarter. I continue to do just as well in my final semester and will graduate in the top 3% of my class with high honors.

- In addition to continued involvement with Teen Line and volunteering at the local animal shelter, my water polo team won our league and finished second in CIF. I started every game and was named 2nd team All-District and Most Improved Player.

List your academic and extracurricular updates in bullet form. Resist the urge to repeat too much information that was in your application. Instead, focus on recent developments.

- I was awarded a "Superior" rating in the Alta Monte Unified School District Science Fair for my project on "Hydroponics: The Future of Agriculture." I will be competing in mid-May at the state level.

I would like to make valuable contributions to the Penn community as a member of the Botany Club as well as continue my volunteer work at a local Philadelphia animal shelter. I also look forward to the opportunity of working closely with professors and conducting original research through the URF program. If there is any additional information I can provide you with, please don't hesitate to contact me

In your third and final paragraph, state that the school is your first choice (if it actually is) and that you will accept a place in the class if you are given a space off the waiting list (if that's true). Thank them for taking the time to consider your application.

at *your email address or your phone number*. Thank you for your careful consideration. Penn is absolutely my top choice for college. If admitted off the waiting list, there is no doubt I would attend as there's no other place I'd rather be.

CHAPTER 9

Adults Only:
How Parents Can Help Without Hurting

Focus on what's really important

Parents, the college admissions process can be a stressful one for you, too. You deserve to enjoy this time with your kids. So to start this section, we're going to share a dirty but effective trick with you.

When we tell groups of parents that one of the most important things they can do to manage college admissions stress is take a deep breath and remember what's really important, we ask them to picture these scenarios.

Imagine making the trip to college with your new college freshman and helping her move into her new dorm room.

Imagine welcoming her home at Thanksgiving, hearing her talk over turkey about how much she loves college, and then rolling out the family red carpet again a few weeks later when she's finally home for the holidays.

Imagine visiting her at Family Weekend, where you meet her new friends and buy yourself a sweatshirt that proudly identifies you as the parent of a college student.

Imagine receiving her phone calls and emails when she tells you how much she's learning, how much fun she's having and how happy she is in college.

Imagine following her progress during college and seeing for yourself how much your former high school senior is maturing.

Imagine hearing her tell you about the professor who sees great potential in her work, the summer internship she's so excited about and how she's finding her passions and thinking about what she'll do after graduation.

Imagine graduation day. You'll think back to changing diapers, to the terrible twos and the elementary school years. You'll remember her braces in junior high and watching her start high school. You'll remember teaching her how to drive, taking pictures before school dances, watching her apply to college and leaving the nest to start life as a college freshman.

Imagine her walking across the stage and accepting her diploma. She's done it. You have raised a beaming, grown-up, happy college graduate.

Now, when you were imagining those things, did it matter whether or not the college was a prestigious one?

We have never once done this exercise and had a parent answer, "Yes."

When you feel the stress of admissions starting to take its toll, just remember that your son or daughter is going to go to college, and someday, you'll be in the audience at graduation. Is anything more important than those two things?

You'll enjoy the college admissions process a lot more if you keep this truism in mind.

Think long term

How would you react if a colleague told you, "I just haven't had much success in my career, but that's because I got a mediocre SAT score."

You'd laugh the guy out of the office. The SAT he took 20 years ago is obviously not the problem. You'd probably feel the same way if he blamed his lack of career advancement on his rejection from Georgetown when he applied at age 17.

During the college planning years, it's easy to assign lifelong importance to things that won't matter even a few years from now. The C+ in French, the SAT score that won't budge or the rejection from a dream school—those things matter today. But the long-term, life-changing opportunity for our kids to go any college—to be better educated, discover their talents, learn, grow, make lifelong memories and have fun while there—that's what matters in the long run.

Going to college is important. But your student's SAT score, grade in math or admissions decision from one dream college won't impact whether she's successful in her career, who she marries or how many grandkids you'll get to spoil one day.

When you focus on the long term, it's easier to see that your kid's work ethic to study like crazy in a physics class he struggles in is more important than whether or not he eventually gets an A.

There are hundreds of colleges that accept almost everyone who applies, so nobody is forcing your hand to make the process more stressful than it needs to be. Like most milestones in your kids' lives, this time will pass quickly. You get to decide how to approach it.

Decide to enjoy it, and you probably will. It's up to you.

Treat rejections like high school breakups

If your daughter came home in tears and told you her boyfriend broke up with her, would you think she was now going to be alone forever? Would you strategize about what she could change to win him back?

We doubt it. You'd tell her how wonderful she is, and the boy who rejected her is a dope who obviously doesn't understand what he's missing. You'd remind her that another boy—the right boy—will see the same great qualities that you do.

That's exactly what to do if a college says, "No."

Some parents react to college rejections by second-guessing the approach their kids took, wondering what would have happened if the test scores had been higher or if the essay topic had been different.

They want to appeal the rejection and claim that other students who were admitted were less qualified.

We understand disappointment. But wallowing in disappointment will only make kids feel worse and delay their opportunity to find a better match.

They blew it

If a college rejection arrives, the best thing you can do as a parent is to tell your student you think the offending college blew it, and there are plenty of other collegiate fish in the sea. Then encourage your student to move on to one of the colleges who had the foresight to offer her a spot.

It's your job as a parent to model the right behavior in the face of disappointment. It may feel devastating, but anyone who's suffered legitimate hardship would tell you that Princeton saying "No" is not a tragedy. Lots of kids are denied admission to their first-choice schools. None of the ones we've worked with are still hurting when they make friends in a dorm someplace else.

Buy the Sweatshirt

Parents, want to show your kids you're excited about their final college choice? Get yourself a sweatshirt that proudly bears the name of the college.

If the sweatshirt actually has the word "mom" or "dad" on it (like, "NYU Mom"), that's even better.

A parent who's decked out in her kid's new school colors vividly tells the world just how proud she is of her soon-to-be-college freshman. Your kids might feign embarrassment when you wear it in public. That's fine. Deep down, they'll be beaming, too.

Some names you may recognize of people rejected by their first-choice colleges:

- Warren Buffett

- Meredith Vieira

- Ted Turner

- Steven Spielberg

- Tom Brokaw

They turned out okay. Your student will, too.

Temporary disappointment is normal, but like a breakup, the faster you can move on, the better. 🎓

Endearing:

Ten Secrets of "Great Kids"

_Charisma isn't everything__. It actually makes a difference to have substance. And those quiet people can be incredibly easy to miss in college admissions, but they can be brilliant and wear incredibly well over the long haul._[1]

William Fitzsimmons
Dean of Admissions
Harvard University

CHAPTER 10

Endearing:
Ten Secrets of "Great Kids"

Cultivate greatness

"He's a great kid."

That's just about the best thing you can have a parent, teacher, counselor, coach, boss or admissions officer say about you.

When people call you a great kid, they're almost never referring to your SAT scores. Being a great kid has more to do with your character—how you treat other people, the impression you make and your maturity, etc. Being a great kid can make all the difference when you're trying to get into college.

The more personal a college makes its admissions process, the more important it is for applicants to be likeable, especially if it's a competitive school. If the straight-A student with high test scores comes off as arrogant, if his letters of recommendation don't mention anything about how much his teachers actually enjoyed having him in class, if he writes an essay that makes weak excuses for the B he got his sophomore year, he just doesn't sound likeable.

Likeable students tend to stay likeable once they get to college.

We see the importance of likeability play out every year at Collegewise. When a student repeatedly shows up late to our meetings and never apologizes, or seems to think he's smarter than all of his classmates and isn't afraid to declare so, or makes fun of awkward kids, we know our office isn't the only place he's doing those things. Those students are never as successful in the admissions process as the great kids are.

In this chapter, we'll share 10 traits great kids seem to exhibit. We would never suggest you change who you are to try to get into college. But these are life skills that will serve you long after you leave high school.

Many people took a lot longer than twelve grades of school to learn some of these. Consider this your opportunity to get a head start.

Meet people well

People make judgments about you within the first few seconds of meeting you. We all do it. It's just human nature. So why not give yourself an advantage and start strong?

Meeting people well and making a good first impression is one of the more important skills you can have. It sets a tone. For example, when a family visits one of our offices for the first time, we can't help but make judgments about their student based on how well he meets us. If he steps forward, looks us in the eye and smiles, shakes our hand and says, "Hi, I'm <insert name>—nice to meet you," we get the impression the kid has his act together.

On the other hand, if he shuffles forward meekly, looks at the ground, and offers us a handshake that resembles a lifeless salmon, he might as well have told us, "I have the personality of a lifeless salmon."

Smile

When you meet someone, smile. Look the person in the eye when you introduce yourself. Offer a firm (not crushing) handshake. It's easy to do, and you'll be pleasantly surprised how positive the impression you make for yourself can be in just three seconds before you've even started a conversation.

Whether you're meeting a fellow student, the new tennis coach, the boss at the store where you want a part-time job or the Duke representative who's visiting your school, if you meet them well, you get to build on a great first impression rather than having to rebuild from a bad one.

Write good emails

Today's college applicant is likely to communicate over email as often, if not more so, than face-to-face. Just as people size you up when you talk face-to-face, the person on the receiving end of your email is going to make judgments about you based on what you write and how you write it. Here's a checklist to review before you email anything to an admissions officer, teacher, counselor or anyone else with whom you want to make a good impression.

1. **Make the subject line something descriptive.**

"Question" isn't descriptive. "Question about how to get involved at your center" is.

2. **Address the person by name at the beginning. Looks like: "Hi, Ms. Harrington:"**

Imagine if someone walked up to you and just started asking you a question without even first saying, "Hi." Wouldn't it be rude (and a little weird)?

3. **If the person doesn't know you or may not remember you, identify yourself in the first paragraph.**

"I met you last weekend at your son's baseball game (my brother David is on the same team). You mentioned that you might need some summer help at your office and asked me to email you."

4. **Keep your email to one screen.**

Don't write something so long they have to scroll through it.

5. **Observe the laws of punctuation, capitalization and good grammar.**

Nobody ever looked stupid for sending a properly capitalized and punctuated email, but they have looked that way for ignoring the rules. This is not a text message.

6. **Don't ever type in all caps.**

When you write "PLEASE RESPOND TO ME ASAP," it reads like you're yelling at the person (or hopped up on espresso).

7. **Be careful with exclamation points for the same reason.**

"I really hope you can write my letter!" sounds like you're yelling.

8. **It's okay to write like you talk as long as you're respectful.**

"The purpose of my email is to request your assistance with my college applications" is too formal.

"I'm writing to ask you if you might be able to help me with my college applications" gets the job done.

9. **Use a normal font.**

Think black type and normal size. No bright colors, cursive, blinking lights, or animated creatures of any kind.

10. **If you're asking for something, say "please."**

11. **At the end, always say, "thank you."**

12. **Proofread carefully.**

13. Type your full name at the end of the message.

If you need a reply back, leave a phone number, too, so the person has the option of calling.

14. Use cc sparingly.

Especially if the person you email doesn't know the people you cc. Imagine if you walked into this person's office and didn't introduce the two people you brought in tow.

15. Are you angry?

Be careful sending an email to someone who's made you angry. "You can always tell a guy to go to hell tomorrow," said Warren Buffet, CEO of Berkshire Hathaway and one of the richest people in the world. "You don't give up that opportunity."

Once you put your anger out there, it's there. You can't take it back. So write it, but don't send it. Come back tomorrow and read it again. If you're still comfortable with what the email says, then send it.

Remember peoples' names the first time

Here's a quick way to make anybody you meet like and respect you more: remember their names after you meet them the first time.

When you meet someone new and you remember his or her name, they notice.

When you use their name during your first conversation ("How long have you played in the marching band, Kevin?") and you remember it the next time you see them, it's like giving them a compliment. It shows you pay attention and care enough to remember their name. You're demonstrating your willingness to make the effort.

When you interview for a part-time job and you say to the boss at the end of the interview, "Thanks so much for your time, Mr. Dillinger," you show your potential boss you pay attention to details.

When you meet the new kid at school and introduce him to your friends, "Hey guys, this is Jason," you'll see the wave of relief wash over the new kid's face now that people actually know who he is.

When you're introduced to a group of two or three people at a time, see if you can remember—and use—all of their names. It's not a coincidence that the few people who actually make the effort to do this are always the ones with the most friends.

Popular excuse

A lot of people say, "I'm really bad with names." But that's just an excuse for not actually trying to remember. Dale Carnegie, late author of the best-selling book *How to Win Friends and Influence People*, compares remembering names to any other skill (e.g., learning to ski). Your progress depends on how important it is to you to do it.

Three of Carnegie's tips for remembering names:

1. Focus on the name when you're introduced, and ask the person to repeat it if you don't hear it clearly.

2. When you are introduced to a person, repeat the name immediately. Don't just say, "I'm Kevin," in return. Say, "Hi Tony, I'm Kevin."

3. Use the person's name during your conversation together.[2]

So make the effort. Practice it. And if you forget a name, it's okay. Just own up to it and say, "I'm really sorry, but I don't remember your name. Can you remind me?"

That's a lot better than trying to fake it every time you run into the person again.

Learn from failure and move on

Most successful students—and adults—have experienced failure. If you put yourself out there enough times to go after things that aren't easy to achieve, you're going to fail every now and then. There's no shame in it, especially if it's a good failure.

If you try out for the varsity volleyball team and get cut, it's not fun. But that doesn't mean it's a bad failure. Maybe you use that free time to do something else you're excited about? Maybe you use getting cut as motivation to come back even stronger next year? Maybe you find a way to be a part of the team anyway by being the team manager, taking photos of the games or running the fundraiser? Any of those scenarios turns that failure into something good.

One of our most successful applicants at Collegewise wrote her essay about how she had lost every election she had ever run in…badly. But she used each of those opportunities to find activities that were even better suited to her. She ended up at Notre Dame.

Sure, not all failures are good. We're not suggesting you should blow off studying for your biology midterm just so you can experience failure. That would be a bad failure. But if you try your best, things don't work out and you take something productive from it, that's a good failure. Don't be ashamed about it.

Here are a few steps to help you turn a failure into a something positive in the long run.

1. Accept your failure gracefully. Don't blame anyone else or get too down on yourself.

2. Think about what you've learned from the experience. Is there something you could have done better or differently, or did this failure point out that your talents might be better put to use elsewhere?

If you're not sure, ask for advice from someone who observed your attempt.

3. Decide a next step. Is there another way to stay involved or contribute? Are you going to improve and come back strong for another try? Are you going to try something else you might be better suited for? Wallowing won't turn this experience into something valuable. Learn as much as you can, and then decide on your next step.

It takes a mature, confident person to admit defeat and to move on positively.

Nobody, including colleges, expects you to be perfect. In fact, most people will be impressed by good failures.

COMMITTEE NOTES

Learn from failure

I've spent enough time in high schools to know teenagers will never be perfect. They do silly things, mess up, fall down and lack confidence. The ability to bounce back is a fundamental life skill students have to learn on their own. The lessons of failure can't be taught in a classroom; they are experienced and reflected upon.[3]

Angel B. Perez
Dean of Admissions
Pitzer College

Accept responsibility

Some people have an excuse for everything. Nothing is ever their fault.

In high school, it's the kid who says he got a C in history because the teacher didn't like him, not because he just didn't study as much as he should have. It's the football player who says he isn't a starter because "it's all political," not because the kid who got the starting nod works harder.

Sure, there are times when something happens to you that really is not your fault. Other times, you're just making excuses. If you're not sure which one it is, use the $1 million scenario.

When we have a student who repeatedly misses or arrives late to meetings or classes but always seems to have an excuse (e.g., "traffic," "too busy" or "I forgot"), we ask, "What would you do if you knew you'd win $1 million if you arrived at your next meeting on time?"

The student inevitably says something like, "I'd leave earlier to beat traffic," or "I'd write it down so I wouldn't forget."

The $1 million scenario exposes when you're making excuses for things that you really could do if you wanted to.

That shouldn't push you to do things that will make you unhappy. If there were $1 million riding on you getting a 4.0 this semester, but in order to do it, you'd have quit the jazz band you love and sleep three hours a night, that's not improving your life. But when you eliminate excuses, you take responsibility for what you do and don't do. You get out of your own way.

Recommend yourself

One college once asked applicants to write a letter of recommendation for themselves. It was a big reach school for a Collegewise student who started his letter, "There is no doubt about it, Joey is an underachiever. He didn't have a learning disability. He didn't have a problem at home. He didn't have bad teachers who didn't care about him. He just didn't work as hard as he should have in high school. But there is more to Joey than his 2.65 GPA..."

He was admitted.

Excuses rarely make someone like and trust you more. Excuses don't work on colleges, either. Make fewer excuses. Take more responsibility.

Learn to apologize well

Sometimes we do things that hurt or inconvenience other people, even if we don't mean to do it. When that happens, forgiveness comes a lot faster if you apologize like you mean it.

A half-hearted "Sorry about that" is not a good apology. That's like an airline telling delayed passengers, "We regret any inconvenience this may have caused."

Does anyone ever feel a lot better after a company says that?

A real apology is sincere. There's emotion to it, which conveys you actually feel bad.

If you break curfew and your parents waited up until 2:00 A.M. wondering where you were, give them a good apology. "Mom, I'm really sorry I made you worry last night. If I had to wait up until 2:00 A.M. worrying if you were okay, I'd be really upset. I should have called you."

If you goof off in class and your teacher has to discipline you, stop by after class and offer up a good apology. "Mr. Cunningham, I'm really sorry I was talking so much in class today. I know it's not easy to teach trig to a room full of 40 kids. I won't do it again."

Even if something wasn't your fault, you can still give a good apology. If you're supposed to meet a friend to study and your softball practice runs too late, just apologize well. "I'm so sorry I never showed up for our meeting. My practice ran late and my coach wouldn't let me get to my phone to call you. I can't believe I left you waiting for 45 minutes."

None of us can go through life without occasionally doing things we have to apologize for. When it happens, apologizing well can actually improve your relationship with the person you let down. It shows that you care about how you treat people. Anybody can do it.

Laugh at yourself regularly

Successful people always have some missteps along the way. The most likeable of them aren't afraid to talk about those times. They share those stories openly and even laugh at themselves when something embarrassing happens. They know that's a much healthier approach than wallowing in embarrassment and hiding from those opportunities in the future.

Let's say you decide to run for student body president and your speech doesn't go well. You lost your place a few times. The joke you thought was supposed to be funny didn't go over well at all. And you ended up suffering what you're sure was the most lopsided loss in school history.

You have two options.

1. You could be morbidly embarrassed, resolving never to put yourself in that situation again, and replaying the loss over and over again in your mind and getting mad at your friends if they ever mention it.

2. Or you could laugh at yourself.

You could joke that it's hard to lose your place twice when the speech is only three paragraphs long.

You could sarcastically tell your friends that you won't be able to hang out with them as much because prominent politicians are asking you to run their campaigns. You could tell your hockey teammates you have great news—due to your absolutely terrible showing in the election, you'll have even more time to work on your slap shot next year.

Picking the second option lets you get over the loss faster. It lets you recognize you tried your best and be proud that you at least took the risk to run for something only two other people at your school had the guts to run for. And it will almost certainly make people like you even more.

Psychology study

Ursula Beermann of UC Berkeley and Willibald Ruch of the University of Zurich studied 70 psychology students to test their ability to laugh at themselves. The findings showed that the ability to laugh at yourself linked with having an upbeat personality and good mood, and may be the foundation for a good sense of humor.[4]

One of our students worked over the summer as an ocean lifeguard in Laguna Beach, California. He wrote his college essay about his first day on the job, a hot Saturday when the beach was packed to capacity.

A group of swimmers had gotten caught in a riptide and were yelling for help. As he climbed down from his lifeguard tower, he tripped and fell eight feet, face first into the sand. He was still spitting sand out and regaining his bearings when he finally got to the water.

This student still laughed about it when he told the story six months later. He even wrote one of his college essays about the face plant and titled it, "Save your-selves!" He got into almost every college he applied to.

When you can laugh about a failure, a weakness or something that was outright embarrassing, it's endearing. It shows confidence and how comfortable you are just being yourself. People love hanging out with others who are like that. Colleges love those people in their classes and dorms.

Give off positivity

"Be positive" can be hard advice to follow. Some people are just naturally a lot cheerier than others. You can't be expected to radically change your personality if it's not your style to skip down the hallways at school every day.

But anybody can make a choice to *give out* positivity—to be complimentary, thankful and congratulatory.

If you really enjoyed a class, tell your teacher. If your teacher stayed after school to help you, tell her how much you appreciated it and how much good it did you. If your teacher helped you with your college essay, read over a rough draft and gave you good feedback or offered you any good advice that really helped you, thank her.

If you got a low grade on a test and your parents were understanding and supportive, tell them how much it helped you to know they were in your corner. If your parents helped you through a situation where you needed guidance, thank them and let them know how much you benefitted from their advice. If they cheered you on when you had a big success, tell them how much their praise meant to you.

Congratulate the members of the cross country team when they win the league championship, the cast of the school play when they close out their final performance or the writer on the school newspaper who wrote a particularly good article you appreciated.

If one of your friends was there for you in a time of need the way we all need a good friend to be every now and then, let your friend know the support didn't go unappreciated.

Be sincere

We're not saying you should lavish thanks and praise on everyone for no good reason. It doesn't mean anything if you aren't sincere.

Heartfelt positivity is free to you and so ridiculously easy to give if you're conscious about it. It will make you feel good about your relationships with people in your life. And it will go a long way toward making people want to be there for you again in the future.

Rise above the drama

Some parts of high school are wonderful. Other parts, not so much—like the popularity contests, social backstabbing and insecurities. It's rough out there. But you actually get to choose whether or not to engage in it.

In our experience, the more you avoid drama, the more it will avoid you.

Try not to worry too much about all the drama that goes on in high school. Just be yourself. Be confident. Don't worry about what other people think. Reject the idea of popular versus unpopular. Be proud of who you are and what you stand for. Do what you want to do rather than what other students say you should.

It's never a good idea to invest too much emotional energy into something that just doesn't matter. You know all the drama about who's popular and who's not, who gets invited to the right party and who gets left home, who looks right or wrong, and all the other bad drama that's so rampant in high school? Nobody will care about any of it once you get to college. In fact, pretty much everyone looks back on it and realizes just how silly all of it was.

Have you ever heard your parents make fun of someone based on what that person did or wore back in high school? Probably not. People grow out of it.

When you go to your ten-year high school reunion, the roles you used to play will be ancient history. The former popular kids and the former social outcasts will all be part of the same club—adults trying to make it in the world.

Until then, just try to stay out of the drama as much as you can.

Nice is underrated

The word "nice" has such an undeservedly bland connotation in high school. Referring to someone as "nice" is like saying, "Well, he's not awful."

It's too bad, because nice is just about one of the best things you can be.

Everybody likes the kid who's genuinely nice. Nice kids are good to their friends and family. They don't make fun of other people or hesitate to say "Hi" to the socially less fortunate. They're easy to trust and hard to criticize. There will probably never be a time in your life after high school when just being nice will make such a difference for people around you. And it's something you can do every day.

Tell people at the junior prom that they look great.

Say "Hi" to your English teacher in the hallway.

Congratulate the kid who beat you in the election.

And for that one poor soul who's the easy target, the one who always gets laughed at and maybe even bullied, pull him aside or send him an email saying, "Those kids are as*holes. I'm so sorry about what they're doing. Keep your chin up."

Extra help

Nice kids get extra help from teachers and counselors when they ask for it.

They get more glowing letters of recommendation from teachers and counselors and make better impressions on college interviewers. Nice kids are more likely to have people in their corners, ready to work and lobby and fight on their behalf. They've earned those benefits by just being good to other people.

When he could tell that the new exchange student from France was having a hard time fitting in at school, one Collegewise student, David, went out of his way to introduce the new student to people and make him feel welcome, going as far as to set him up with a date for the spring formal. David's English teacher mentioned his efforts in her letter of recommendation as an example of the kind of great kid that David was.

He went on to attend one of his reach schools, Santa Clara University.

Being nice is free and easy. And it gives you a chance to impact a lot of people without really having to do much. And even though there's no place to list "I'm a nice kid" on a college application, all the nice kids we've worked with always seem to end up with plenty of college options. 🎓

11. Parting Words

" **College has been** the most amazing experience of my life so far. I joined a sorority, started writing for the school newspaper and even spent this last year studying abroad in London and Athens. I really feel like I have grown up in college, but the responsibility isn't something that weighs me down; it's what I love about it. I couldn't wait to get out of high school, but I never want college to end! "

Katie S.
Former Collegewise student, class of 2006
Pepperdine University

CHAPTER 11

Parting Words

Find college memories

Congratulations—you're done with this book. We hope you're excited to find the right colleges for you, and to have a little fun while you're at it.

Your college process deserves to be taken seriously, but the families who enjoy this time the most care less about the name of the college and more about the experiences their kids will have once they get there.

There are plenty of great colleges out there. The challenge is finding and eventually deciding on the schools that fit. You now have all the knowledge you need to find, apply, get in and pay for those schools that fit you. We now invite you to put those lessons to work, so you can start enjoying a defining four years in college.

In college, you'll take classes you actually want to take. You'll learn from professors who have dedicated their professional lives to one particular subject and are willing to share their knowledge with you. Every single day of your college career, you'll learn something—maybe from a professor, maybe from a friend or maybe from a meaningful experience. That means every morning you wake up, you'll be a little bit smarter than you were the day before.

You'll go to good parties.

You'll date—a lot.

You'll meet more new people and make more friends than you've ever made before. Some of those friends will be in your life forever. Some will stand at your wedding one day. Some will one day tell your kids how you both pulled an all-nighter together in your dorm studying for your chemistry final.

College memories have a long shelf life.

Your college memories

There likely will be an experience in college—one you may not recognize when it happens—that you'll look back on when you're 40 and realize how important it was. It might be the class that makes you realize just how much you love literature.

It might be the professor who takes the time to tell you she sees great potential in your work.

It might be an internship, time you spend abroad or the day you meet the person you'll eventually marry.

Whatever it is, your defining memory is out there waiting for you at your future college.

Now, you have to go make it.

Defining memories aren't limited to the schools atop the U.S. News & World Report rankings. They can be found at more than 2,000 four-year colleges out there. You're most likely to find your memories at the right college, the place where all your college soul searching, the college visits, your counselor and just plain gut instinct told you to go.

The right college is the one that fits you.

That concept is why The Princeton Review began publishing our Best College guides. It is a founding principle of Collegewise. Our strong shared belief in finding the right colleges had a lot to do with how our companies came together. It's why we spend so much time trying to convince students (and their parents) to stop worrying about getting into what they think are the best colleges and start working on finding the ones that fit them best.

The right school is out there waiting for you. Go find it.

Best of luck with your college admissions journey.

Relax. It will be okay. You're going to enjoy it. 🎓

Acknowledgements

This book would not exist without the hard work, help, and support of the following people:

Adam Kleiner (editor of the first version), Rosie Bancroft, Roger and Claudia McMullin, Allison Cummings, Arun Ponnusamy, Paul Kanarek, Katie Konrad Moore, Deborah Ellinger, and all our Collegewise counselors.

Thank you to the hundreds of thousands of students over the years, who have completed The Princeton Review's annual surveys, sharing their college experiences and allowing us to help high school students find their best fit schools.

And to the Collegewise students and parents who trusted us, let us ride shotgun on their rides to colleges and allowed their stories to be shared here, thank you. Keep wearing those sweatshirts proudly.

About the Authors

Kevin McMullin is the founder and head of counseling at Collegewise, a college admissions counseling company that became part of The Princeton Review in 2012. A popular public speaker, Kevin has given over 500 presentations at high schools and conferences to discuss smarter, saner college admissions planning. As long as the speeches don't require him to do any math problems, he always does a bang-up job. Kevin is a graduate of UC Irvine with majors in English and history and earned his college admissions counseling certification from UCLA. He also writes a daily college admissions blog at www.wiselikeus.com.

Robert Franek oversees The Princeton Review's guidebook publishing program—a line of more than 150 titles from best-selling test-prep guides to college, graduate school, career-related reference books. As the company's chief expert on higher education issues, he directs The Princeton Review annual surveys of college, business school, and law school students upon which the well-known Princeton Review rankings are based. As lead author of the company's annual *Best Colleges* guide, he has appeared on NBC's *Today* as well as programs on ABC, CBS, CNN, FOX, and NPR, among others. He visits more than 50 colleges a year and has been a lecturer and panelist on college admissions for audiences of educators, parents and students. Prior to joining The Princeton Review in 1999, Robert served as a college admissions administrator at Wagner College (Staten Island, NY) for six years. He earned his BA at Drew University in political science and history.

Basic Retraining:
How to Approach the College Admissions Process

1   Parsishbeachpatrol, "Reality Check: I love you just the way you are," Swarthmore College Admissions: The Blog, September 28, 2007, Swarthmore College, parrishbeachpatrol.wordpress.com/2007/09/28/reality-check-i-love-you-just-the-way-you-are/

2   Blake Ellis, "Harvard, Princeton post record low acceptance rates," CNNMoney, March 30, 2012, http://money.cnn.com/2012/03/30/pf/college/acceptance_rates_ivy_league/index.htm

3   Caroline M. Hoxby, 2009. "The Changing Selectivity of American Colleges," *Journal of Economic Perspectives*, vol. 23(4), pages 95-118, Fall.

4   Hoxby, "The Changing Selectivity of American Colleges."

5   "Myth: It's impossible for regular students to get in anymore," University of Wisconsin, Madison, accessed April 19, 2012, http://www.news.wisc.edu/admissions/myth6.html

6   Jay Mathews, "10 Ways to Survive 11th Grade," *Washington Post*, April 11, 2006, http://www.washingtonpost.com/wp-dyn/content/article/2006/04/11/AR2006041100484.html

7   United States Department of Labor, Bureau of Labor Statistics, College Enrollment and Work Activity of 2010 High School Graduates, April 8, 2011, http://www.bls.gov/news.release/hsgec.nr0.htm

8   Malcolm Gladwell, *Outliers: The Story of Success* (Little, Brown and Company, 2008), 48.

9   Internet Movie Database, "Seth Rogen," IMDb, http://www.imdb.com/name/nm0736622/

10   Mark Cuban, "Success and Motivation P4." Blog Maverick: the Mark
     Cuban weblog, May 25, 2004, http://blogmaverick.com/2004/05/25/
     success-and-motivation-p4/

11   Andrew Flagel, "Will hyper-involvement help you get admitted (and would
     that be worth your time)?" Not Your Average Admissions Blog: A Beneath
     the Surface Look At Everything College Admissions (with a few shame-
     less plugs) (blog), June 25, 2010, http://notjustadmissions.wordpress.
     com/2010/06/25/will-hyper-involvement-help-you-get-admitted-and-
     would-that-be-worth-your-time/

12   Tara Parker-Pope, "College's High Cost, Before You Even Apply," *The
     New York Times*, April 11, 2006, http://www.nytimes.com/2008/04/29/
     health/29well.html?_r=1&ref=health&oref=slogin

13   Vivian Giang and Eric Goldschein, "Killing Elephants, Space Travel, Running
     Marathons: What 12 CEOs Do In Their Spare Time," *Business Insider*,
     February 23, 2012, http://www.businessinsider.com/here-are-12-crazy-
     activities-ceos-do-in-their-spare-time-mark-zuckerberg-bob-parsons-
     2012-2?op=1#ixzz1nKwVM0zG

14   Zimbio, "Hidden Talents of Politicians," accessed June 26, 2012, http://
     www.zimbio.com/Hidden+Talents+of+Politicians

15   Kaja Perina, "The Genius of Play," *Psychology Today*, January 01 2003, http://
     www.psychologytoday.com/articles/200301/the-genius-play

16   Ben Jones, "There is no formula," MIT Admissions (blog), MIT, December 16,
     2004, http://mitadmissions.org/blogs/entry/there_is_no_formula

17   Parrishbeachpatrol, "Reading season: a brief explanation," Swarthmore
     College Admissions: The Blog, Swarthmore College, March 4,
     2010, http://parrishbeachpatrol.wordpress.com/2010/03/04/
     reading-season-a-brief-explanation/

18   Sandy Baum, Jennifer Ma, Kathleen Payea, "Education Pays 2013: The Benefits
     of Higher Education for Individuals and Society," College Board. Accessed
     October 8, 2013, http://trends.collegeboard.org/sites/default/files/educa-
     tion-pays-2013-full-report.pdf

Finding Fits:
How to Find the Right Colleges for You

1   Robert Samuelson, "Prestige Panic," *Newsweek*, August 2006, http://www.thedailybeast.com/newsweek/2006/08/21/prestige-panic.hml

2   Peter Ewell, No Correlation: "Musings on Some Myths About Quality," *Change Magazine*, November 2008, http://www.changemag.org/Archives/Back%20Issues/November-December%202008/full-no-correlation.html

3   Seth Godin, "Do elite trappings create success? (Causation vs. correlation)," December 20, 2010, http://sethgodin.typepad.com/seths_blog/2010/12/do-elite-trappings-create-causation.html

4   "Undergraduate Colleges," Harvard Law School, accessed June 26, 2012, http://www.law.harvard.edu/prospective/jd/apply/undergrads.html

5   "Fortune 500: Our annual ranking of America's largest corporations," CNNMoney, accessed June 26, 2012, http://money.cnn.com/magazines/fortune/fortune500/2012/full_list/

6   Clinedinst, Hurley, and Hawkins, "2011 State of College Admission." NACAC, November 2011. http://www.nacacnet.org/research/research-data/Documents/2011SOCA.pdf

7   "The 7 Most Common Schools For Google And Apple Employees," Huffington Post, March 29, 2012, http://www.huffingtonpost.com/2012/03/29/where-did-google-apple-college_n_1387567.html#s822713&title=Stanford_University

8   Gayle B. Ronan, "College Freshmen Face Major Dilemma," MSNBC, November 29, 2005, http://www.msnbc.msn.com/id/10154383/ns/business-personal_finance/t/college-freshmen-face-major-dilemma/#T4I_8dmiYoM

9   "Undecided Major," Marquette University, accessed June 26, 2012, http://www.marquette.edu/explore/major-undecided.shtml

10   Malcolm Gladwell, What College Rankings Really Tell Us, *The New Yorker*, February 14, 2011, http://www.newyorker.com/reporting/2011/02/14/110214fa_fact_gladwell

11   Justin Pike, "Love your list," Inside Admissions: Behind the scenes with Tufts admissions officers, Tufts University, October 21, 2011, http://admissions.tufts.edu/blogs/inside-admissions/post/love-your-list/

Preparing:
How Any Student Can Become a More Competitive College Applicant

1   "Our selection process, Academic Preparation," Stanford University, accessed June 26, 2012, http://www.stanford.edu/dept/uga/basics/selection/prepare.html

2   "Important Factors in Admission to JMU," James Madison University, accessed June 26, 2012, http://www.jmu.edu/admissions/process/freshman.shtml

3   "Preparing for College," Vanderbilt University, accessed June 26, 2012, http://admissions.vanderbilt.edu/facts/preparing-for-college.php

4   "Applying to Ole Miss/Freshmen," University of Mississippi, http://www.olemiss.edu/admissions/fap.html

5   Parrishbeachpatrol, "Making the Best of High School,"Swarthmore College Admissions: The Blog, Swarthmore College, January 19, 2010, http://parrishbeachpatrol.wordpress.com/2010/01/19/making-the-best-of-high-school/

6   Andrew Flagel, "A in Regular or B in Advanced Placement," Not Your Average Admissions Blog: A Beneath the Surface Look At Everything College Admissions, October 27, 2007, http://notjustadmissions.wordpress.com/2007/10/27/a-in-a-regular-or-b-in-advanced-placement/

7   Kaiser Foundation, "Generation M2: Media in the Lives of 8- to 18-Year-Olds," 20 January 2010, http://www.kff.org/entmedia/entmedia012010nr.cfm

8   Marcel Adam Just, Timothy A. Keller, Jacquelyn Cynkar, "A decrease in brain activation associated with driving when listening to someone speak," Center for Cognitive Brain Imaging, Department of Psychology, Carnegie Mellon University, February 19, 2008, http://www.distraction.gov/research/PDF-Files/carnegie-mellon.pdf

9   Department of Transportation, "Driver Distraction in Commercial Vehicle Operations, Federal Motor Safety Administration," September 2009, http://www.distraction.gov/research/PDF-Files/Driver-Distraction-Commercial-Vehicle-Operations.pdf

10   Cal Newport, "Anatomy of an A+: A Look Inside the Process of One of the World's Most Efficient Studiers," Study Hacks: decoding patterns of success, May 18, 2011, http://calnewport.com/blog/2011/05/18/anatomy-of-an-a-a-look-inside-the-process-of-one-of-the-worlds-most-efficient-studiers/

11   Jean Johnson, Jon Rochkind, Amber N. Ott and Samantha DuPont, "Can I Get a Little Advice Here? How an Overstretched High School Guidance System Is Undermining Students' College Aspirations," A Public Agenda Report for the Bill and Melinda Gates Foundation, Public Agenda, March 3, 2010, http://www.publicagenda.org/files/pdf/can-i-get-a-little-advice-here.pdf

12   Clinedinst, Hurley, and Hawkins, "2011 State of College Admission," page 31.

13   Ibid.

14   BBC Television, "Horizon," 1981.

15   Tom Rath, *StrengthsFinder 2.0*, (New York: Gallup Press, February 2007).

16   Shane Lopez, *The Encyclopedia of Positive Psychology*, (Wiley-Blackwell, August 2011).

17   Rath, *StrengthsFinder*, page iii.

18   Wendy Livingston, "Overheard in Committee: What Happens in Committee Doesn't Stay in Committee," Admit It! True Confessions from W&M's Admission Officers, College of William and Mary, February 29, 2012, http://blogs.wm.edu/2012/02/29/overheard-in-committee-what-happens-in-committee-doesnt-stay-in-committee/

19   Jose Antonio Vargas, "The Face of Facebook: Mark Zuckerberg opens up," *The New Yorker*, September 20, 2010, accessed June 26, 2012, http://www.newyorker.com/reporting/2010/09/20/100920fa_fact_vargas

20   "Tips for Writing a Great Essay," University of Michigan, accessed May 3, 2012, http://www.admissions.umich.edu/essays/tips

21 Valerie Strauss," Question 3: Do colleges want well-rounded students or those with a passion?" *Washington Post*, November 3, 2009 http://voices. washingtonpost.com/answer-sheet/college-admissions/question-3-do-colleges-want-we.html

22 Greg Roberts, "The Rumor Mill," The UVA Admissions Blog: Notes from Peabody, February 17, 2012, http://uvaapplication.blogspot.com/2012/02/rumor-mill.html

23 Strauss, "Question 3."

24 Strauss, "Question 3."

25 Strauss, "Question 3."

26 Strauss, "Question 3."

27 "The Happy Wackiness of Zappos.com," ABC News, October 26, 2011, http://abcnews.go.com/blogs/business/2011/10/the-happy-wackiness-of-zappos-com/

28 Strauss, "Question 3."

29 Jessica Godofsky, M.P.P.; Cliff Zukin, Ph.D.; Carl Van Horn, Ph.D; "Unfulfilled Expectations: Recent College Graduates Struggle in a Troubled Economy," Worktrends: American's Attitude about Work, Employers, and Government," John J. Heldrich Center for Workforce Development, Rutgers University, May 2011, http://www.heldrich.rutgers.edu/sites/default/files/content/Work_Trends_May_2011.pdf

30 Charles Fishman, "Face Time With Jeff Bezos," *Fast Company*, January 31, 2001, http://www.fastcompany.com/magazine/43/bezos.html

31 "Q. and A.: College Admissions," *The New York Times*, December 17, 2008, http://questions.blogs.nytimes.com/2008/12/17/qa-college-admissions/

Testing:
Planning and Preparing for Standardized Tests

1   Matt McGann, "What's the big deal about 40^2?" MIT Admissions, November 20, 2004, http://mitadmissions.org/blogs/entry/whats_the_big_deal_about_402

2   Drawn from multiple sources including:

Dan Fletcher, Brief History: Standardized Testing, *Time*, December 11, 2009, http://www.time.com/time/nation/article/0,8599,1947019,00.html

"Where Did the Test Come From? A Brief History of the SAT," Frontline: Secrets of the SAT, PBS, accessed April 27, 2012, http://www.pbs.org/wgbh/pages/frontline/shows/sats/where/history.html

Ida Lawrence, Gretchen W. Rigol, Thomas Van Essen, and Carol A. Jackson, "A Historical Perspective on the SAT 1926-2001," The College Board, 2002, http://professionals.collegeboard.com/profdownload/pdf/rr20027_11439.pdf

Examined Life, http://www.gladwell.com/2001/2001_12_17_a_kaplan.htm

"History of the ACT," American College Testing, accessed April 16, 2012, http://www.act.org/aboutact/history.html

"History of the Tests," The College Board, accessed June 4, 2012, http://sat.collegeboard.org/about-tests/history-of-the-tests

John Cloud, "Should SATs Matter?" *Time*, March 4, 2001, http://www.time.com/time/nation/article/0,8599,101321,00.html

3   "National Merit Scholarship Program," National Merit Scholarship Corporation, accessed June 24, 2012, http://www.nationalmerit.org/nmsp.php

4   "Prepare for College Level Studies," The College Board, accessed October 18, 2013, http://professionals.collegeboard.com/k-12/prepare

5   "Fee and Liability Policies," The College Board, accessed October 18, 2013, http://www.collegeboard.com/sss/help/feesandliability/basicuserfee/index.html

6   Clinedinst, 2011 State of College Admission.

7   Robert S. Clagett, "Middlebury Dean Says SAT or ACT Score Is 'Seldom a Deal Breaker,'" *The New York Times*, October 15, 2010, http://thechoice.blogs.nytimes.com/2010/10/15/middlebury/

8   "Test Optional," Lawrence University, accessed June 21, 2012, http://www.lawrence.edu/admissions/about/testoptional.shtml

9   "Test Optional Frequently Asked Questions," Sewannee University, accessed May 28, 2012, http://admission.sewanee.edu/apply/test-optional-frequently-asked-questions/

10 "10 Myths about the SAT," Fairtest: The National Center for Fair and Open Testing, August 20, 2007, http://fairtest.org/10-myths-about-sat

11 "Issues in College Success: The Relative Predictive Validity of ACT Scores and High School Grades in Making College Admission Decisions," ACT, 2008, http://www.act.org/research/policymakers/pdf/PredictiveValidity.pdf

12 "The ACT: Biased, Inaccurate, and Misused," Fairtest: The National Center for Fair and Open Testing, August 20, 2007, http://www.fairtest.org/facts/act.html

13 Cloud, "Should SATs Matter?"

Applying:
The Art of College Applications

1   Angel B. Pérez, "Want to Get Into College? Learn to Fail," *Education Week*, February 1, 2012.

2   Ben Jones, "It's More Than A Job," MIT Admissions, MIT, March 17, 2006, http://mitadmissions.org/blogs/entry/its_more_than_a_job

3   "Hot Chicken and Data Days," Undergraduate Admissions Blog, Vanderbilt University, February 24, 2009, http://admissions.vanderbilt.edu/vandybloggers/2009/02/hot-chicken-and-data-days/

4   Clinedinst, 2011 State of College Admission.

5   Clinedinst, 2011 State of College Admission.

6   "Q. and A.: College Admissions," *The New York Times*, December 17, 2008, http://questions.blogs.nytimes.com/2008/12/17/qa-college-admissions/

7   Peter Schworm, "College applications can be too good: Admissions officers wary of slick essays," *Boston Globe*, February 12, 2008, http://www.boston.com/news/education/higher/articles/2008/02/12/college_applications_can_be_too_good/?page=full

8   William Honan, "Personal Essay Questions: Turning Torture Into Fun," *The New York Times*, December 27, 1995, http://www.nytimes.com/1995/12/27/us/personal-essay-questions-turning-torture-into-fun.html?pagewanted=all&src=pm

9   Parke Muth, "Writing the Essay: Sound Advice from an Expert," Office of Undergraduate Admission, University of Virginia, accessed June 27, 2012, http://www.virginia.edu/undergradadmission/writingtheessay.html

10 Schworm, "College applications can be too good."

11 Valerie Strauss, "Admissions Officials Tell What They Like (and Don't Like)," *The Daily Gazette*, May 5, 2002, http://news.google.com/newspapers?nid=1957&dat=20020505&id=Q-EqAAAAIBAJ&sjid=E4oFAAAAIBAJ&pg=4091,1288889

12 Code of Medical Ethics of the American Medical Association, "Opinion 8.19 - Self-Treatment or Treatment of Immediate Family Members," June, 1993, http://www.ama-assn.org/ama/pub/physician-resources/medical-ethics/code-medical-ethics/opinion819.page

13 Bryan G. Nance, "I've Got 99 Problems... Admissions Is Not One," MIT Admissions, MIT, October 25, 2005, http://mitadmissions.org/blogs/entry/ive_got_99_problems_admissions

14 Martha C. Merrill, "Note to Applicants: Admissions Officers Do Read What Your Teachers Say," *The New York Times*, October 8, 2010, http://thechoice.blogs.nytimes.com/2010/10/08/teacher-rec/

15 Evan Cudworth, "Phoenix Tip #2: Letters of Recommendation," The Uncommon Blog, University of Chicago, September 6, 2011, https://blogs.uchicago.edu/collegeadmissions/2011/09/phoenix_tip_2_letters_of_recom.html

16 Greg Roberts, "It's Time to Focus," The UVA Admissions Blog: Notes from Peabody (blog), University of Virginia, February 2, 2012, http://uvaapplication.blogspot.com/2012/02/its-time-to-focus.html

17 Tamar Levin, "A Warning: Colleges Can Change Their Minds," *The New York Times*, March 18, 2009, http://thechoice.blogs.nytimes.com/2009/05/18/a-warning-colleges-can-change-their-minds/

College Interviews:
What to Expect
When You're Face-to-Face

1   Parsishbeachpatrol, "The College Interview," Swarthmore College Admissions: The Blog, Swarthmore College, September 4, 2009, http://parrishbeachpatrol. wordpress.com/2009/09/04/the-college-interview/

2   Clinedinst, 2011 State of College Admission.

3   Dave Marcus, "Advice for the College Interview: Girls, Dress Discreetly; Boys, Mind Those Hands," *The New York Times*, October 25, 2010, http://thechoice.blogs.nytimes.com/2010/10/25/october-interview/

4   Steve Cohen, "Do College Interviews Really Count?" *Forbes*, October 10, 2011, http://www.forbes.com/sites/stevecohen/2011/10/10/do-college-interviews-really-count/

5   "Arrange an Interview," Carleton College, Admissions, accessed June 27, 2012, http://apps.carleton.edu/admissions/interview/

6   "Interviews for Freshmen Applicants," Yale University, Admissions, accessed June 27, 2012, http://admissions.yale.edu/interviews

7   "Prospective Students Visiting Campus," Admissions, Claremont McKenna College, accessed June 27, 2012, http://www.claremontmckenna.edu/admission/visit/

8   John DeTore, "Thoughts On The MIT Interview," MIT Admissions, MIT, October 19, 2006, http://mitadmissions.org/blogs/entry/thoughts_on_the_mit_interview

9   Malcolm Gladwell, *What the Dog Saw*, (New York: Little, Brown and Company, 2009), 381-382.

10 Jenni Laidman, "Making an Impression," *Toledo Blade*, June 25, 2001, http://cjonline.com/stories/062501/pro_impressions.shtml

Affording College:
How to Get Financial Aid and Scholarships

1   "Saving for College," FinAid, accessed June 27, 2012, http://www.finaid. org/savings/

2   Mark Kantrowitz, "College Q&A: How Early Is Too Early to Start Saving?" Main St., November 10, 2010, http://www.mainstreet.com/article/ moneyinvesting/education-planning/college-qa-529-or-trust-account-0

3   "The Real Deal on Financial Aid," Muhlenberg College, accessed June 28, 2012, http://www.muhlenberg.edu/main/admissions/realdeal.html

4   "Number of Scholarships," FinAid, accessed June 28, 2012, http://www. finaid.org/scholarships/awardcount.phtml

Deciding:
How to Handle Admissions Decisions and Pick Your College

1   Valerie Strauss, "Why Students Get Rejected from College," *Washington Post*, March 26, 2010, http://voices.washingtonpost.com/answer-sheet/college-admissions/college-rejection-its-not-abou.html

2   Clinedinst, 2011 State of College Admissions.

Adults Only:
How Parents Can Help without Hurting

1   Lucia Graves, The Perils and Perks of Helicopter Parents, *US News*, December 18, 2007, http://www.usnews.com/education/articles/2007/12/18/the-perils-and-perks-of-helicopter-parents

2   Jeanine Lalondem, "Family roles during the application process," The UVA Admission Blog: Notes from Peabody, University of Virginia, December 28, 2011, http://uvaapplication.blogspot.com/2011/12/family-roles-during-application-process.html

3   Judy Fortin, "Hovering Parents Need to Step Back at College Time," CNN, February 4, 2008, http://articles.cnn.com/2008-02-04/health/hm.helicopter.parents_1_helicopter-parents-college-students-students-with-higher-levels?_s=PM:HEALTH

4   Dr. Terri LeMoyne and Dr. Tom Buchanan, "Does 'Hovering' Matter? Helicopter Parenting and Its Effect on Well-Being," *Sociological Spectrum*, July/August 2011, http://blog.utc.edu/news/2012/01/professors-study-effects-of-helicopter-parenting/

5   Ibid.

6   "'You've got to find what you love,' Jobs Says," Stanford Report, Stanford University, June 14, 2005, http://news.stanford.edu/news/2005/june15/jobs-061505.html

Endearing:
Ten Secrets of "Great Kids"

1   Rebecca R. Ruiz, "The Ideal High School Graduate," October 27, 2011, *The New York Times*, http://thechoice.blogs.nytimes.com/2011/10/27/ideal-grad/

2   "Quick and Easy Ways to Remember Names," Dale Carnegie Training, accessed June 27, 2012, http://www.dcarnegietraining.com/resources/remembering-names

3   Perez, "Learn to Fail."

4   American Psychological Association, Ursula Beerman and Ruch Willibald, "Can people really laugh at themselves?"—Experimental and correlational evidence, http://psycnet.apa.org/index.cfm?fa=buy.optionToBuy&id=2011-11794-003, (June 2011).

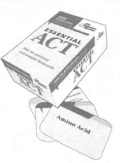

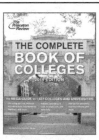